That's My Business!

Alton Douglas

[Type here]

Published by Saron Publishers in 2025

Copyright © 2025 Alton Douglas
Cover design © 2025

All rights reserved
No part of this publication may be reproduced, stored in a retrieval system, or transmitted, in any form or by any means, without the prior permission in writing of the publisher, nor be otherwise circulated in any form of binding or cover other than that in which it is published and without a similar condition including this condition being imposed on the subsequent purchaser

ISBN-13: 978-1-913297-65-7
Also available as an ebook
978-1-91329766-4

Saron Publishers
Pwllmeyrick House
Mamhilad
Mon
NP4 8RG

saronpublishers.co.uk
info@saronpublishers.co.uk
Follow us on Facebook and Twitter

That's My Business!

Alton Douglas

[Type here]

For more of Alton's books
visit
altondouglas.co.uk

Acknowledgements

My thanks to so many friends: They back me up with their laughter and even, occasionally, buy one of my books.

Keith Price: Who looks after the tech stuff (everything that scrambles my brain).

Jo: She has checked every word I've written and still, at this late stage, finds me reasonably amusing.

You: Whoever you are – that's if you are not already on the way to the nearest charity shop to unload this tome.

Any errors in this publication are not of my making. Blame them on my teachers, who are long past caring,

Alton Douglas

In the 50s and 60s there was a proliferation, particularly in the North, of magazines designed to cover clubland activities. The Entertainment Secretary, an extraordinary character, it would seem purely bred for that purpose, would book artistes and then, amongst other things, write about their performances:

As you know we do not allow bad language in our club. I was very pleased that the comedian refrained from using any at all until I came to pay him.

I tried to book 'Singers Anonymous' but nobody seemed to know who they were.

There have been accusations that some of the artists' money has been siphoned off and shared with the sole agent for the club - and I am very upset about this - I can say honestly that I have never shared any of it with the agent.

I told the mind reader exactly what I thought of him but he said that wasn't at all necessary.

The girl singer seemed very full of herself. My wife thought that was true of her dress as well.

I don't think the ventriloquist was really trying. His dummy did most of the talking.

Some of the turns have complained about the dressing room. I don't know how many times I have told them that we hope to have one eventually.

I have to explain to new members that 'Free and Easy' does not apply to all our barmaids.

I apologised to the stripper, after Sunday's lunchtime stag show, for bursting into the dressing room when she was fully clothed.

That's My Business

It was a shame about the highwire act. His new assistant should have told him that she suffered from vertigo.

I asked the accordionist how he learned to make it look so easy. He said he used to have a job folding road maps.

As members will recall, there was an accident, on Saturday, when the magician asked for a volunteer to take part in his 'sawing a woman in half' routine. The Chairman's wife can be visited, in the Accident Hospital, in Wards 8 and 10.

I have asked the agent to stop substituting acts every other week. A lot of hard work goes into the preparation of the posters and we are running out of chalk.

We will definitely not be booking The Chippendales again after one of their number showed his annoyance.

Tickets for our big Xmas raffle can now be obtained from George Armstrong's Marbella address.

Speaking personally I can't stand that hypnotist but for some reason I always rebook him when he's finished.

I am pleased to announce that our reinforced stage will be back in time for next week's concert but we will not be booking any more heavy metal groups.

We held a two-minute silence to mark Fred Turnbull's passing. I am sure he would have loved it.

Alton Douglas

ARMY DISORDERS

That's My Business

During my six weeks' National Service basic training in Catterick in 1958, I can remember one lad whose posture was, well, to be polite, not exemplary. He was crossing the parade ground one morning and I heard the Sergeant Major, scream, 'That man there, you look like a f------ dromedary!'

-.-.-.-

Our Bandmaster, in the 5th Royal Inniskilling Dragoon Guards, was not always the most considerate of leaders. However, he did once have a rush of blood to the head. We finished a long and gruelling recording session in Cologne at 3am and he said, 'Right, you can have the rest of the night off.' Night?

-.-.-.-

On a lengthy trip, in the back of a lorry, to one of our bookings we started cracking puns - something I'm quite good at. So good, in fact, that the other members of the band threatened to lower the tailboard and deposit me on the autobahn.

-.-.-.-

Whenever we played late at night, at the Officers Mess or a dance, we were supposedly supplied with a meal in the cookhouse. Most times the cookery experts were missing and we had to fend for ourselves. The best meals I ever had, in my two years, were cooked up by a bunch of starving musicians in the early hours!

-.-.-.-

In the regiment there was someone, whose real name I never knew, who was known as 'Buffet'. He was the only soldier, as far as I can remember, who kept carpet slippers by the side of his bed. He was very popular with certain officers.

Alton Douglas

YOU'RE IN THE ARMY NOW

That's My Business

If ever there was a non-military person in a military uniform it was me during my National Service days. Then, as now, I stayed reasonably sane by writing about my experiences - mainly in joke form:

The Sergeant has told me that I've been assigned to General Duties, along with Corporal Punishment and Private Parts.

The bloke in the next bed is ignorant. He thinks that being 'Put on fatigues' means an extra hour in bed.

When he left home to start his National Service his wife said the Military Policemen seemed very friendly.

Told him to khaki and blanco all his kit - now he can't get into his shirt.

He's gone AWOL so often they've booked him reserved accommodation in the Guard Room.

'That man there - if you spent as long cleaning your rifle as you do reading books you'd have the enemy really worried.'

'And when you see an Officer you always have to salute. Longest way up, shortest way down.'
   Wouldn't it be simpler just to shake hands?'

'None of our pants, green cellular, have come back from the laundry, Sarge.'
   'That's all right - you'll have to swap with one another.'

Supposedly true: A young and relatively inexperienced Corporal, given the onerous task of demonstrating a new weapon, was understandably nervous. 'Everybody in the room, this morning, out-ranks me – fortunately no one knows as much as I do.'

Alton Douglas

MUSINGS OF A MUSO

That's My Business

I had only been out of the Army a few days when I was approached by a local musician. 'I understand that you want to get some experience of working gigs. I can't afford to pay you with my trio but you can sit in if you like and I'll occasionally give you 10 bob out of my money.' I accepted and enjoyed the opportunity until, one day, I cottoned on to his game. He was charging for the four of us and then splitting my quarter with the other two. That was that.

Actually, I don't feel any bitterness towards him because it had been invaluable experience. I had learned so many things to do, and not to do, when you front a band, which I was able to put into practical use when I formed my quartet shortly afterwards.

-.-.-.-

Trouble in the matrimonial home! In those fledgling days of my quartet, the wife of one of my musicians noticed that night, when he was undressing, that his Y-fronts, which had been worn as prescribed that morning, were now showing the label on the outside. Oh, dear!

-.-.-.-

Over the next few years the line-up changed considerably until, in 1967, Billy Forrest, the agent, suggested that we turn professional. We talked it over, auditioned successfully, gave up our day jobs and accepted a six month season at the Derbyshire Miners' Holiday Camp, in Skegness. The money was not brilliant - £100 between four and Billy's 10% to pay - but none of us could resist it. I decided that the only thing was to pay in terms of need:
　Paddy Ryan: drummer, had six children.
　Adrian Barnby: our pianist, had three.
　Aloysius Donaghy: bass, had a wife who was expecting their first child.
　Me: bandleader, trombonist, vocalist and, at that time, single.
　Everybody was satisfied and, despite the leader getting the worst financial deal, I didn't mind at all. I knew then that it was the gateway to my progressive career – even if I had no idea where it was leading me.

Alton Douglas

STRIKE UP THE BAND

That's My Business

The 15th October 1976 was the day that respected Midlands' bandleader, Norman Dovey, achieved one of his lifetime ambitions - an hour's broadcast with his big band. BBC Radio Birmingham had asked me to compère the programme, something I was delighted to do, particularly as it was their very first stereo broadcast. Fast forward thirty years and his daughter contacted me to say she had been listening again to a recording of our show and she thought it was such a pity I had chosen to take the mickey out of her Dad! I was stunned for a second and then mentally retracked. Norman and I had met at a photo shoot for the *Radio Times* publication as part of an intended double page feature. As we met we both burst into laughter at the disparity in our heights - Norman, I would say, was about 5'6" and I was, and still am, 6'1". We both agreed, there and then, that we would model our dialogue on another programme we both enjoyed featuring Roger Moffat and the Northern Dance Orchestra, in which banter played a big part. So there were references to the difference in our height (with at one point me claiming that I was by far the shorter person). The whole hour was claimed to be a major success and it cemented a very good relationship. His daughter apologised for her interpretation and we parted friends.

The incident confirmed a long-held belief of mine that many people don't understand banter. It is probably a masculine form of humour – good-humoured leg-pulling between men who like each other. I discovered, in my Army days, that the only people who were not subjected to it were those who were not well liked!

I have remembered another incident. Because studio time was very expensive, Norman had to cram a lot of rehearsal into the relatively short allotted period. Suddenly one of the trumpet section, Roger Siviter, announced, 'Brothers, as you all know, union rules dictate how long we practise. We have already gone over that time.' Norman was, to say the least, gobsmacked. He snapped, 'Okay lads, take a break.' He turned to me. 'It's only taken me twenty years to get this broadcast. I thought it would be good not only for me, as a bandleader, but for local musicians. We've only got half an hour left now and he plays the union card. Unbelievable!'

Alton Douglas

MUSICAL NOTES

That's My Business

Musicians are frequently the creators or the subjects of humorous chat:

After hearing my band someone said I should be known as 'The Leader of the Banned.'

'There were so many deps in our band, last night, I wasn't even sure who I was.'

A pianist, gritting his teeth after accompanying a female singer with a face mummified with botox injections, said, 'It was bit like playing at a tribute to the taxidermists' art.'

'That wedding reception we played at finished up as a free-for-all. The bride's side won by a knockout.'

'It's always so cold in that club that my regular piano player wears mittens. It sounded as if the bloke I used last night was wearing boxing gloves.'

'They're mad at dancing at that place. A waiter dropped a tray and two couples got up and started dancing.'

'I reckon to qualify for a heavy metal group you have to prove you've got tin ears.'

'That drummer has got no sense of timing whatsoever - he arrived for Saturday's gig on Sunday.'

'The Aussie banjo player has demanded a pay rise. I think he's addicted to plonk.'

Alton Douglas

THE BAND CALLS

That's My Business

'The Band Call' is the name given to the rehearsal period artistes would have before starting a one nighter, week or season at a venue. Most times the backing groups were of a very high standard but, just occasionally, you would come up against snags. As it was such a rare occurrence, I thought you might like to hear of a handful of single night engagements where I abandoned the idea of including music in my act altogether:

The strangest set-up I have ever seen was in a small upmarket restaurant in the North, where the duo were on a platform suspended above the tiny stage. When they struck up it was as if Thor had decided to take vengeance on mankind. I thanked both of them profusely but, for the sake of my eardrums, gave them a lengthy break.

-.-.-.-

I arrived for the opening night of a brand new nightclub in the West Country, to find just a drummer waiting for me. I knew the owner was inexperienced in the business but this was a first. 'Excuse me, but where's the keyboard player?' He looked bemused. 'I didn't think you'd need one. You play the tune and he backs you.' With the Mayor arriving to open the place shortly after, I shrugged and remained music-less.

-.-.-.-

It's a long way to travel for a one nighter on the Isle of Wight but just once, when the till rang in my head, I did undertake one. It turned out to be a very nice hotel, free accommodation provided, but the organist was not only bad tempered but musically inadequate. I patiently tried to talk through my simple 'dots' but he might just as well have been reading the local newspaper. After several attempts to play three numbers adequately, I gave up and suggested perhaps it would be better if I coped without any backing. He was furious. 'Listen, mate, I'm a very important man on this island. You'd do best not to fall out with me!'
I left early the next morning before the Mafia arrived.

Alton Douglas

THE ALMOST-JOLSON STORY

That's My Business

As a lad I was captivated by the singing of Al Jolson after seeing the bio-pics *The Jolson Story* and *Jolson Sings Again*. However, the story doesn't end there:

Norman Brooks was a Canadian Jolson impersonator but what particularly thrilled me was to hear a voice that was magically like the real thing but singing modern songs. You couldn't have anything more up-to-date, at the time than the lyric to *My 3D Sweetie*. I bought several of his hit records, including *A Sky Blue Shirt and a Rainbow Tie* and *Hello Sunshine*. To this day I think he was as near to the real Jolie as you could get.

-.-.-.-

I was booked to appear on a Saturday London Town Hall bill with Al Jolson's son. However, the night before, he was exposed on a radio show as a fraud and we were both thrown out of work.

-.-.-.-

Larry Parks, who played the singer in both the films, came to Birmingham's Hippodrome with his wife the actress, Betty Garrett. Their act was just a run-of-the mill song and dance performance but we could have forgiven that if he had made just a reference to the films.

-.-.-.-

Birmingham had its own Al Jolson in Billy Manns who earned quite a living in the late 60s around the local clubs. At that time, Christmas was a frantic period for all us artistes and sometime we would do two or three dates in one night. I remember seeing Billy in his little van tootling of to another booking in full Jolson black face make-up. I often wondered if the police ever stopped his van, only to be confronted with a pseudo Jolson.

Alton Douglas

JUST A THOUGHT

That's My Business

When I was in digs in Blackpool in 1969, I had a landlady who could out-malaprop Mrs Malaprop. If there was a way of strangling our language she would find it. So I thought I would include some of her beauties along with a collection of varied quotations:

'I've got a problem with me drains. Got them people coming today to do 'em. You know the ones - Dynamo.'

'I hate this damp weather. Every morning I come down and my windows are covered by compensation.'

'The next door neighbour says he's the one who gave him a description for his consternation.'

When the regular pianist with my quartet was on holiday, I employed an experienced musician who said at the end of the first night, 'I can't work it out. I reckon you are one of the worst musicians I've ever worked with - and the best bandleader.'

If ever there was a better dismissal of all the hard work involved, I have never yet encountered it. After one cabaret, a man came up to me and opened with, 'It's money for old rope being a comedian. All you've got to do is to make people laugh.' (I was tempted to show him the scars.)

In the world of literature you are just as susceptible to comments. After reading some of my Showbiz comments in my books and on Facebook, someone wrote to me to complain. 'You seem to do an awful lot of bragging about the famous people you've worked with - and there's the over-familiarity in using their Christian names.' Well, what he didn't seem to realise is that, when you work in theatre, cabaret, radio and television, these people are your workmates!

(I remember, when I did my very first warm-up for *The Golden Shot,* Bob told me off for calling him 'Mr Monkhouse'.)

Alton Douglas

BITS ABOUT THE BIZ

That's My Business

This is a true story. A comedian friend was having an affair with his own doctor's wife. I said to him, 'That's a bit risky, isn't it?' His reply was a peach. 'I only see her during visiting hours.'

-.-.-.-

George Bartram, the Birmingham publicist for so many well-known acts including Morecambe and Wise, Tony Bennett, Vince Hill and Little and Large, was celebrated for his reliability. He told me once that he wanted, on his headstone, the words, 'He always rang back.'

-.-.-.-

Jo and I were asked to perform the opening ceremony for a furniture shop in Rugby. The company was opening a whole series of them simultaneously all over the country. That morning, for the first time, we met Ron Ryan. He played guitar and sang during the course of the day. It wasn't until years later, when I read his autobiography, *Crash, Bang, Wallop* that I discovered that he had written most of the numbers recorded by the Dave Clark Five

-.-.-.-

I did a lot of work for one agent for several years. One of the jobs was an annual show at the Palace Theatre, in Redditch. Shortly afterwards he rang me and said, 'They would like to book you again for next year.' I said, 'I'd be delighted but you'll have to ask for a bit more money - that fee was much lower than I normally get.' He came back to me. 'I'm sorry but they just can't afford a penny more.' I thought for a moment. 'Okay, I will do it.' The show was a great success but when I came to be paid the organiser said, 'That was great but hasn't your fee gone up!' The next morning I rang the agent. 'You told me there was no more money and I find you are making 10% and another £10 on top of that.' He retorted, 'Don't you tell me how to run my business!' I said, 'I'm not - I'm telling you how not to run mine!' Could there have been others?

Alton Douglas

FELLOW WORKERS AT THE COALFACE

That's My Business

Two of my friends, sadly no longer with us, also worked as television warm-up comics. 'Warming up' is not necessarily an easy job. You have to create a happy atmosphere before the show begins and then fill in any breaks in the recording. With *The Golden Shot*, the fill-ins were very brief because it went out live but some programmes had extremely lengthy gaps. When I worked on *The Peggy Lee Show* she had been very ill and she had to be taken in a wheelchair to the dressing room for her costume changes - for the only time, I should think, in television history, I let the audience go out to the loo - fortunately they all came back!

Felix Bowness: I always thought that he was the King of the warm-up comedians with, literally, thousands of shows to his credit, including *This Is Your Life*, *The Morecambe and Wise Show* and *The Two Ronnies*. In his early days Felix was a bantam weight boxing champion. Towards the end of his life he was seen on the screen regularly as Fred Quilley, the ex-jockey, in *Hi-de-Hi*.

-.-.-.-

Dave Ismay: Dave was the warm-up comic for *The Golden Shot* in its first years and became a close friend of Bob Monkhouse. However, after a while, he found the trip down from the North every Sunday was too much and that's when I came into the picture in 1972.

In 1981 Norman Vaughan devised a programme called *Bullseye* as an intended vehicle for himself. The TV high-ups loved the concept but not Norman as the presenter. He then suggested that I should do it but 'No', I wasn't well known enough. They settled on Dave. The director, Peter Harris, went to see him in his home, explained the format and exactly when it would all kick off. The story goes that Dave said, 'I'll just go and get my diary and make sure I'm available.' When he came back into the room Peter had gone. Such is the vanity of some television people.

Jim Bowen was the next choice - he accepted, presented it for 14 years and, in the process. it is reputed, became a millionaire.

Alton Douglas

Tony Christie turned out to be one of the nicest people in the business. We were in digs together at Richard Linley's in Sunderland in 1968. At that time he was the lead singer with Tony Christie and the Pen Men.

I spent an afternoon searching for his wife's contact lens (we eventually found it in the sink waste pipe). The last time I saw him was at the Al Martino concert at the Lichfield Garrick Theatre in 2008. Al told the audience that their local hero was in the audience and he was given a well-deserved round of appreciation. (You'll remember that, on its revival, Tony had had a big hit with the song *Is This The Way To Amarillo*.) Tony continued to perform for a while despite suffering from dementia.

-.-.-.-

The American singer, **Billy Eckstine**, was at the Birmingham Hippodrome in 1956. I was a little bit disappointed, having read about him in a jazz reference book, that he didn't play trumpet or valve-trombone, but his musicianship was more than reflected in his singing. In those non-PC days he was known as the 'Sepia Sinatra' and the curled shirt collars he wore led to the fashion catching on in this country. I was just walking past the stage door as he came out to be greeted by a group of his fans. I overheard one girl shout, 'I couldn't have got any closer to him.' Her friend giggled, 'You could have!'

-.-.-.-

In the early 50s I remember seeing the singer, **Ronnie Harris**, who had had quite a hit with *The Story of Tina* on a Hippodrome bill. After that, very little was heard of him over the following years. In 1968, the agent Billy Forrest booked me for a tour of military bases in Germany and Italy, culminating in a show at the Allied Officers Club in Naples with the legendary American vocalist, Billy 'That Old Black Magic' Daniels'. The agent at the German end of things was none other than Ronnie Harris.

That's My Business

Tommy Bruce was an artiste I enjoyed working with. We were together in *Stars and Garters* at Barnsley Civic Hall and laughed our way through the entire week. I particularly loved his versions of his hit recordings, *Ain't Misbehavin* and *Chantilly Lace*, sung in what he described as his 'sandpaper and gravel voice'. I did always wonder, and never heard from anyone, how he fared in some of the Welsh clubs where purity of voice was always considered a major asset!

-.-.-.-

A husband and wife team, **Vic Odin and Louise**, whose act comprised strong man effects and magic, told me that they were going through a bad patch, finding work scarce. I rang a contact I had in the Bailey organisation and they booked them up for a thirteen-week tour of their venues. At the end of the run they both came round to see me, thanked me profusely, explaining that it had been a career life saver - he then asked me if I could lend them enough money to get home!

Alton Douglas

WRESTLING WITH MY PAST

That's My Business

The world of wrestling is so far removed from my comfort zone that I cannot imagine, for a second, how I came to like three of its exponents!

Sid Millard: Sid was the first drummer with my band in 1960. He soon decided there was more appeal in becoming an all-in wrestler. He and his wife, the singer Jean-Anne, agonised over what name he should use. His given name did not have the right appeal, they felt, and wracked their brains for an alternative. Eventually he said to me. 'Can you think of anything?' I stared disbelievingly back at him. 'Sid, it's so obvious - "El Sid"!'

-.-.-.-

Farmer Johnny Allan: Appearances can be deceptive. I was reminded of him last week watching an episode of *Last of the Summer Wine*. You may remember a scene with him and Foggy Dewhurst, set in a pub, where Foggy demonstrates in his usual confident, totally incompetent manner, how to disrupt things by destroying Johnny's Rubik Cube. He and I were characters in ATV's series *Muck and Brass*. We had scenes together at Walsall Football Club, a hotel in Leicester and in the Birmingham studios and got on famously. Talking to this gentle, considerate man it was hard to imagine that he was once the British and European Middleweight Champion.

-.-.-.-

Pat Roach: Pat was a very successful wrestler who branched out into the world of acting. He appeared in such movies as *A Clockwork Orange*, the Bond film *Never Say Never Again* and *Indiana Jones and the Last Crusade* but, to most of us, he will always be thought of as 'Bomber' in four series of television's *Auf Wiedersehn, Pet*. He opened his own gymnasium in Birmingham, at the time I was writing my fortnightly Showbiz column for the *Northfield Messenger*, so it seemed the perfect chance to interview him. He was extremely affable, we got along very well and when we'd finished he said, 'I enjoyed that. I'd like to take you out for lunch.' He did - we had a delicious takeaway cheeseburger!

Alton Douglas

SEEING DOUBLE

That's My Business

I was in digs in Sunderland in 1968 with Eddie McGinnis. He was one of a double act called Sid and Eddie and he and his partner had to find separate accommodation because their then-wives didn't get on. Eddie was great fun but now and then I saw his serious side. Apparently, he was always being advised to get rid of Sid and go solo. That night, finishing early, I went to see their nightclub act and thought Sid was a very, very good straight man. Fortunately they did stay together and went on to top the bill in summer seasons and pantos, eventually starring in several of their own television series. By this time their management had insisted on a name change and they had become Little and Large.

I told Eddie that Earle and Vaughan, after seeing me adapt my act for afternoon children's shows during a week in Cleethorpes, had dubbed me 'Uncle Alton'. After that Sid and Eddie would only call me that!

-.-.-.-

The re-christening had taken place the previous week. Kenny Earle told me that, some years before, Malcolm Vaughan, who was a very fine singer, had recorded *St Theresa of the Roses* and, selling over half a million copies, had split with him to go solo. During the break Kenny worked as a Kleeneze door-to-door salesman. However, just as with Sid and Eddie, they came to the conclusion that they were better together.

When Showbiz started its slow decline in the 70s, Kenny went on to work as a booker for London Management. He rang me one day to say, 'I've just seen your ad in the *Stage* newspaper - it's not a good idea to put "no sole agent", it looks as if no one is interested.' I said, 'The wording was deliberate. I had a management deal when I started and found it too restrictive. I want to pick and choose my bookings for myself.' He pondered for a second. 'Okay, well, I may be able to pass a few jobs on to you.' Thanks very much, Kenny - I'm still waiting.

Alton Douglas

THE SEEDS ARE SOWN

That's My Business

In the late 1940s, '50, and '60s Birmingham had almost an embarrassment of theatrical riches and as soon as the war years were over we went as often as we could afford:

Birmingham Repertory Theatre: The first purpose-built repertory theatre in the country had in its company in the early 60s, an actor that the consensus of most theatregoers felt was destined for great acclaim. He became Sir Derek Jacobi.

One of the plays that Jo and I enjoyed was NF Simpson's *One Way Pendulum* and on holiday, seeing the film version was at a local cinema, arrived to find it had been withdrawn. So many people had protested and asked for a refund that they had no choice!

In 1989 I was at the Rep, for a week, in *Wanted One Body*.

-.-.-.-

Alexandra Theatre: We grew to be very fond of the rep company and, in later years, I had contact with two of the members. My only day's work as an Extra involved a couple of scenes with Tony Steadman in the Alfred Burke TV series *The Public Eye*. I also met up with Derek Royle twice when he contacted me to see if I would like to write the libretto for a musical based in the city that he was anxious to write. Sadly, and I have no idea why, the project fell through.

-.-.-.-

Birmingham Hippodrome: This, for me, was the Palladium of the Midlands! More than anything I loved variety shows. The tingle started the moment the pit orchestra struck up. I can remember in particular Frank Sinatra playing to a half empty theatre, Anton Karas (*The Third Man* zither music), The Four Aces and Jerry Colonna (a trombone was passed up from the pit and he played a roistering *I Play Trombone Chicago Style*). Later, I worked with a couple of them - Billy Daniels (I was at the Allied Officers Club in Naples with him) and Max Wall (I introduced him at the real Palladium in my one appearance there). I would always hope that halfway through the first half would be Jimmy James - for me, the funniest comedy act I ever saw.

Alton Douglas

BEFORE IT ALL REALLY KICKED OFF

That's My Business

When I came along it was a great surprise for my parents. They thought they had only put their name down for a council house.

Mind you, it was an even bigger surprise for me!

Mum and Dad were both out at work, all day, so they got me a nanny. I've always been fond of goats since.

In infants' school the teachers had to restrain me from butting the other kids.

I had three siblings – by the strangest coincidence so did they.

I can't claim to have been the brightest of children. I thought the three R's were rough, ready and 'restling.

Absenteeism was always a major problem. Amongst the teachers, that is.
    The School Board man had them on a rota.

I was quite glad to get to the big school where the Head Teacher didn't know the meaning of discipline. Actually, he didn't know the meaning of a great many other words either.

By any standards it was a rough place. Mr Thompson was the only teacher who had all his limbs left after a week.

School outings were something of an adventure. One year they took us to Pentonville to visit the Gym Teacher.

I will always remember my last day there. The Head shook my hand vigorously. I didn't notice, until I got home, that my watch was missing.
    I should have been more cautious – I knew he never had any time for me.

Alton Douglas

ALL A LOAN

That's My Business

During my years in Showbiz I was loaned three items:

Vince Hill: I did quite a lot of theatre dates with Vince and knowing of my interest in clowns, he brought one of his own paintings to show me. It was an excellent portrait of himself in full clown makeup. I was very impressed and he said, 'Why don't you borrow it – it would look nice in your lounge.' It certainly did and I kept it for about six months. I suspect it was painted during the lengthy time Vince and Annie were so determined to have a son or daughter and there was such a sadness in his eyes. Eventually Atholl was born but their joy was short-lived. In his teens he became involved with a drug set and died in his early forties

-.-.-.-

Alan Randall: We worked together on many occasions and his George Formby act was always a tremendous success, although I always preferred his magnificent jazz vibes playing. He arrived at one date with Formby's personal scrapbook and offered to lend it to me. Out of politeness I accepted, although I had never been a fan of the star and I have to say that I never even opened it.

-.-.-.-

Dickie Valentine: After an excellent week together at the Cresta Club in Solihull, Dickie said, 'I'd like to lend you this book that Sid gave me (Sid Boatman was his pianist). I think you'll enjoy some of the gags.' It was a collection of a thousand jokes and toasts. 'You can let me have it back next time we work together.' Sadly Dickie died before I had a chance. When I contacted his widow, Wendy, she said, 'He spoke very highly of you - I'm sure he would have liked you to keep it.'

To this day it has a proud position in my bookcase.

Alton Douglas

PURELY BY CHANCE

That's My Business

Coincidences confuse me. How is it that, with so many things going on all around our planet, some things happen in parallel?

As a youngster my great passion was cricket. Each year, from when I was 11, my mother would send a guinea to Edgbaston to buy a Ladies season ticket - this enabled me to watch all of Warwickshire's county cricket games free (where she got the money from, I can't imagine as she was a widow). So you can picture my delight when I went for my first job interview, to find that the Manager at the Motor Union Insurance Company was Richard Mead-Briggs. He played for Warwickshire C.C.C. in 1946, albeit only a couple of times (at the age of 44).

I was hired as a Junior - which was a polite term for a gofer - and I hated the job. The great bonus was that I met Jo there - 70 years ago!

-.-.-.-

I had two cricketing heroes, one of which was the Warwickshire captain Tom Dollery. I was determined to write an up-to-date biography of him. I contacted his widow, his son David, and the ex-county secretary, Leslie Deakins, who was very keen to be involved. We devised an outline, presented it to the club and received an abrupt 'No!' If they financed a project like that, they felt, all the other ex-captains would expect similar treatment!

I toyed with the idea of a book on my other hero, Eric Hollies, who dismissed Don Bradman in his last Test innings, depriving him of the much-coveted average of 100, but the Dollery experience had put me off. Talking to Jo about it she said, 'I used to be in the same class as Eric Hollies' daughter Jackie!'

-.-.-.-

My brother Maurice was a football referee and I was telling him that I had a brief schoolboy romance with Jackie, the daughter of ex-Birmingham City footballer, Jackie Badham. He said, 'That's funny, I was at a meeting with him last night and I regularly play bowls with his son - whose name is Jack.' At the risk of over-egging the pudding there is a 'Jack' in bowls!

Alton Douglas

My friend, Ken Windsor, flew to New York to stay with his friend, Jill Hawkins. He arrived, worn out by the flight, to be greeted by, 'I'm off shortly to meet another old friend. Would you like to come with me? I think you'd find her interesting.' He declined. 'I'm exhausted and, to use, a Tony Hancock expression, my head feels like two braised lamb chops.' Jill laughed. 'That's a coincidence. The person I'm going to meet is Freda Hancock, Tony's widow.'

-.-.-.-

Jo had a fall in recent years at home and I had to send for the paramedics, only to be told that there a six-hour waiting time. Half an hour later the doorbell rang and a nurse was standing there. I said, 'Oh, I'm so glad to see you.' She looked a bit puzzled, 'I've come to give the Covid vaccinations.' I said, 'Jo is lying on the bathroom floor waiting to be helped up!' She bundled in and we were able to get Jo upright again. Five and a half hours later the paramedics arrived.

-.-.-.-

In the 1980s I did a series of concerts with The Bachelors (minus John Stokes by this time). Being the model of tact, I didn't mention to them that when I arrived in Blackpool for a summer season in 1971, my landlady told me that the occupant of my room, the previous year, had been John.

-. -.-.-

Keith Ackrill's son-in-law, in a conversation with American singer Julie Felix and her manager, mentioned that it was his father-in-law's birthday. Julie said, 'Do take him a signed photo and a copy of my latest CD.' Keith was thrilled with her kindness and the picture went straight into a frame. Some years later he decided to take it out of the frame and transfer it into his scrapbook. The day he transferred it he heard that Julie had passed away that same day.

That's My Business

Another from Ken Windsor. He travelled from Taunton to Harrogate, which necessitated a hurried change of trains in Leeds. Breathles, he flung himself down into a seat at the last minute, only to hear from the seat next to him, 'Hello, Ken.' Sitting there was a fellow member of the National Executive Council for Hospital Radio.

-.-.-.-

David Niven, who was a famous film star before the war, as Lt. Col. David Niven, became Major Glenn Miller's commanding officer during the war. Both their birthdays were on 1st March.

-.-.-.-

It is NOT a coincidence that Alton Glenn Miller and Alton Douglas have the same first name - just keep this between us, please, but he cribbed mine.

Alton Douglas

MORE OF THE SAME BUT DIFFERENT

That's My Business

As far back as I can remember I've loved Jewish humour. Knowing this, so many people fed me jokes. I've mentioned in previous books that my one-time manager, Bertie Green, was a great raconteur and when I was resident in West End nightclubs the customers would supply a fund of them. I was also fortunate in my friendship with the Jewish comedian and actor, Harold Berens.

He once gave me a piece of advice. 'Never dissect a joke to see what makes it funny. You'll ruin it that way.' I asked him, 'What do you do then?' He shook his head, 'As a good Jewish comic I dissect it.'

-.-.-.-

He reckoned he'd been in a café, that morning, sitting opposite another Jewish fellow. Neither of them exchanged a word until suddenly the man let out a loud, 'Oy, vey!' Harold said, 'You're telling me!'

-.-.-.-

'Waiter, this chicken is terrible - fetch me the manager.'
'I shouldn't bother, Sir, he won't taste any better.'

-.-.-.-

'Goldie, next month you and I are going to live in a more expensive apartment.'
'Oh great, Sammy. Does that mean we're moving to a better area?'
'No, dear, the landlord's putting the rent up.'

-.-.-.-

Two men in a rowing boat. Suddenly it overturned and leaves them floundering in the water. One of them shouted, 'Hymie, that's a funny way of swimming - waving your arms about like that!"
'Swimming? Swimming? You fool - I'm talking!'

Alton Douglas

(The scene is a hospital.)
'Good morning, Moishe.'
  'Good morning, Doctor.'
  'Are you comfortable?'
  'I make a living.'
  'My prognosis is that you'll live to be 70.'
  'But I am 70!'
  'Did I lie?'

-.-.-.-

'So, what's the matter with those tablets I've given you?'
  'Since I've been taking them I'm a different woman. My husband prefers her.'

-.-.-.-

I think this could have been one of Harold's, out shopping with his mother as a little boy:
  'Hold my hand. If you get lost, don't come crying to me.'

-.-.-.-

Marriage is like a violin. When the music stops the strings are still attached.

-.-.-.-

A young man lost in the centre of a city stops a Rabbi. 'Excuse me, Sir, how do I get to the University?'
  The Rabbi paused for a moment. 'Study!'

-.-.-.-

'Morris, how is your shop doing in this recession? Everybody wants 2 for 1 today.'
  'Two for 1! I tell them it's 1 for 1 and they're lucky to get it so cheap! I could make it 0 for 1.'

-.-.-.-

'Shirley, when do you think you can pay me for that last delivery of dresses?'
  'Don't ask me - do I look like a fortune teller?'

That's My Business

Myron the tailor never had much luck with his slogans but try he did. 'Nothing is too much trouble.'

-.-.-.-

'He tried again, 'Bespoke Tailors - our suits fit like nothing on earth.'

-.-.-.-

He finally settled for, 'Troubled by your appearance? Come in - we won't laugh.'

-.-.-.-

'That woman said she couldn't understand my dialect.'
　'Don't let it bother you. You should worry more about your accent.'

-.-.-.-

'I'm thrilled to bits. My wife has had her credit card stolen.'
　'Aren't you worried?'
　'No, not at all - the thief's spending less.'

-.-.-.-

'Miltie, before we got married you promised to keep me in the way I was accustomed for the rest of your life.'
　'I didn't know I'd live so long!'

-.-.-.-

'When we were courting, Rachel, how come you told me you were a good cook?'
　'I never did! I said I'd cook you meals you'd never forget.'

-.-.-.-

'I'm not saying you're a bad cook - how can I put it? Let's say you and my stomach don't get on.'

Alton Douglas

'You've been a good Showbiz agent for me through the years - I'd like to repay you.'
   'That's very nice.'
   'So, lend me fifty quid.'
   'I lend you fifty so you can repay me?'
   'Spot on. I can pay you some commission then.'

I was not in the least bit surprised to hear, in response to my humorous books, that so many of you shared my affection for Jewish humour. (Incidentally, I once asked Harold Berens for some gags and he said, 'I wish I had a joke for every one I've forgotten!')

'I've just seen your brother and he looks really miserable.'
   'I know. He's remembered someone owes him a pound and he can't remember who!'
   'Come to think about it, you don't look too cheerful yourself?'
   'I'm worried in case he remembers it was me!'

-.-.-.-

'My wife insisted we go on a cruise, so I went to the bank for a loan. It's the only time in my life when "No" sounded sweeter than "Yes".'

-.-.-.-

'I was a bit surprised to see that sign in your shop window "Come in and see what's free."?'
   'It certainly brings the customers in.'
   'Well, what is free?'
   'Nothing!'

-.-.-.-

'Hymie, you can't go out dressed like that!'
   'If I go out dressed up, beggars ask me for handouts.'
   'But what happens if they see you like that?'
   'They give me handouts.'

That's My Business

'Miltie, how long have you and me been business partners?'
  'Oh, it must be forty years now.'
  'A bit like a marriage then?'
  'I suppose it is. Why?'
  'I want a divorce and custody of the shop.'

-.-.-.-

'When your wife asks if her posterior looks big in her new dress it's best to answer in the affirmative. I've discovered that way they don't speak to you for a week!'

-.-.-.-

'Teenagers these days - my son's a mumbler - I can't understand anything he says. The rabbi reckons he's either got a speech impediment or he's a hit man for the Mafia.'

-.-.-.-

'Sarah, your credit card bill has just arrived. Shall I pour the arsenic?'

-.-.-.-.

'How's business in car dealership these days?'
  'Terrible, terrible. All they want is the oldest, cheapest, second-hand transport they can get. If you know anybody who deals in chariots ------'

-.-.-.-

As ever we find two men marooned on a desert island:
  'Solly, what's the matter with you?'
  'Nothing, I don't know what you mean?'
  'We've only been here an hour and already you're arguing as to who gets the coconut concession!'

Alton Douglas

RANDOM THOUGHTS

That's My Business

Thoughts on drinking: Ex-Black and White Minstrel Tony Mercer, during our summer season in Weston-Super-Mare, was seemingly troubled by my being a teetotaller. He was always the first to buy a round but would insist every time that I ordered his gin and tonic and a coke for me.

The singer, Julian Jorg, said to me once, 'I've never in my life trusted someone who doesn't drink - you are the only exception.'

In the days leading my quartet, the organisers of the dance functions would always send up a round of four pints - not one of my band ever drank beer!

-.-.-.-

Thoughts on dress: Comedian Don MacLean said that, in the 1970s, comics dressed just like pop singers - meaning that we all looked exceptionally outstanding. Nowadays he will have noticed that comics still dress like pop singers but unfortunately now they dress as casually as their audiences.

-.-.-.-

Thoughts on cars: Something I'd never thought about before - I saw an advert for a number plate 'AD 1'. Bells rang. Popping into my local friendly garage I asked the owner Jock if he thought I ought to get it. He looked troubled. 'Is that really you, Alton? Are you that insecure that you need your name on a car? And when you park outside a club anyone interested will know it's yours and you could become a target.' He was right - call it a momentary aberration on my part.

Mind you, I never saw any sign of insecurity with Jimmy Tarbuck and I used to park next to his car, COM 1C at ATV in Borehamwood.

Or Paul Daniels and his MAG 1C.

Alton Douglas

MUCK AND BRASS REVISITED

That's My Business

I'm sorry to introduce a note of mystery but here's another story, 100% true but out of respect for his family, no name. When the producer of ATV's *Muck and Brass* series was interviewing local comics and actors, a group of us were sitting in the foyer waiting to be called. A fellow-comic, well known for being his own Number One fan, walked in and ambled slowly over to the receptionist. She said, 'Name?' He looked absolutely shocked at such a lack of recognition. 'My name?' He turned, walked back to the door and then made a slower, more deliberate walk back to the girl. She looked up and said 'Name?'

(Despite several comics playing characters in *Muck and Brass* - Mel Smith, Tony Kent, Les Wilson, Jim Bowen and yours truly - he didn't get a part.)

-.-.-.-

As most of *Muck and Brass* was shot in Birmingham, in 1982 it was quite natural that the bulk of the Extras were local artistes. Having worked with nearly all of them in the clubs over the years, when we weren't needed for filming I would often sit and swap stories with them. One of them said to me, 'Do you think it's such a good idea, you having a speaking part, that you're seen so often talking to us?' Poppycock!

-.-.-.-

I have touched on this before but I thought I'd risk repeating it (simply because I enjoy the punchline!). Mel Smith, who was playing the leading character, and I got on so well that, when we filmed outside the city, he would insist that I travelled back with him in his chauffeur-driven car. We would spend the whole journey in gales of laughter and even exchanged addresses (incidentally, neither of us ever corresponded with each other after that). On the last day of filming he presented me with a badge which read, 'You are a boring old fart.'

Alton Douglas

DEMOCRATICALLY SPEAKING

That's My Business

The definition of Democracy is, to put it simply, a system by which we get the opportunity to elect those we feel are best fit to look after us. Some of these responses never fail to amuse me:

'The best argument against Democracy is a five-minute conversation with the average voter.' (Sir Winston Churchill)

-.-.-.-

'Democracy is beautiful in theory. In practice it is a fallacy.' (Benito Mussolini)

-.-.-.-

'Democracy is the process by which people choose the man who'll get the blame.' (Bertrand Russell)

-.-.-.-

'Democracy means simply the bludgeoning of the people by the people for the people.' (Oscar Wilde)

-.-.-.-

'The real safeguard of democracy is education.' (Franklin D. Roosevelt)

-.-.-.-

'Journalism is what we need to make democracy work.' (Walter Cronkite.'

--.-.-.-

'Democracy is the worst form of government except for all the others that have been tried.' (Sir Winston Churchill)

Alton Douglas

A STING IN THE TALE

That's My Business

I did countless theatre shows with the highly successful vent act, Keith Harris and Orville, and a week of memorable Oxford one-nighters with a three-handed comedy show that included rural comic, Squire Ronnie Hayward. To my surprise, some years later, I discovered that Keith was also doing a very blue act around University campuses - again with equal success.

-.-.-.-

One of my friends was the impressionist Paul Melba. We met in digs in Bristol and laughed ourselves silly for the whole week. Paul was a brilliant mimic best remembered, to this day, for his frighteningly accurate portrayal of people such as Prince Philip, James Mason and Frank Sinatra. In 1974 he appeared in a Royal Variety Performance. Knowing that, at one time, he was reputed to be earning as much as £2000 a show, I was flabbergasted to hear that that he had died penniless in Spain. According to the newspapers his daughter had to organise crowd funding to pay for his funeral.

-.-.-.-

Andy 'Muscles running to fat' Wade was first and foremost a stag comic who became a male stripper. After much persuasion from his friends, including me, he was finally bullied into retiring from the latter at the age of 60! I suggested to him that he could try being a children's entertainer. Again after a lot of cajoling he learned a few tricks, became 'Magic Andy', had stickers on the side of his car and earned a very good living for over ten years.

-.-.-.-

I bet that never in his wildest dreams would England's cricket fast bowling legend, Freddie Trueman, imagine that his daughter, Rebecca, would marry in 1991 Damon, the son of Hollywood glamour queen, Raquel Welch. Sadly, the marriage only lasted a couple of years.

Alton Douglas

TAKING THE MIKE

That's My Business

Mike Carter was an unusual sound impressionist in that he mainly specialised in effects rather than voices – jet planes, thunderstorms and so on. He never failed to go well but what marred his act for me was his last routine. He would have a very noisy train coming in to a station, there would be a slight pause and then an Asian voice (you could do that in those days) would shout, 'Mind those bloody doors!' We did a week together at the Cresta Club in Solihull and I said to him, 'Mike, you never swear in your act - why use that word in your last gag? It will get just as big a laugh without it.' He said, 'Okay, I'll give it a try.' The next night he did and finished to almost complete silence!

-.-.-.-

Jo and I went to see a one-man show at the Malvern Theatre. Although we had never heard of him we were intrigued at the thought of Mike Goddard doing a complete solo performance as Tony Hancock. He was brilliant and we just had to go backstage to congratulate him. That same year, 1969, I was booked as Principal Comic in a revue at the South Shore Casino in Blackpool. Our show didn't start until most of the other shows had completed their first house so I was delighted to see that Mike was with *The Danny La Rue Show* at the Opera House which gave me a chance to say 'Hello' to him before it began. Imagine my surprise when, at one point, Danny looked down Toni Palmer's cleavage and said, 'I'm just looking for Alton Douglas!'

Mike, apart from being a very fine impressionist, has had quite a varied life being, amongst other things, a boxer and a jockey.

-.-.-.-

The British Magical Society held their 76th Annual Dinner at Penns Hall, in Sutton Coldfield. My friend Mike Gancia recommended me as the Guest Speaker and compère for the evening and I was booked by Mike Lines. The latter, 40 years later, sent me a DVD of the event, complete with my speech. Brace yourselves - and I can be seen using a mic (different spelling, I know, but pronounced 'Mike'!).

Alton Douglas

GYM'LL FIX IT

That's My Business

I am seriously thinking of joining a gym. That's probably enough exercise for this week.

I've now decided to take the plunge and join up. I might as well have a heart attack somewhere warm.

In the past you'd just need a T shirt, a pair of shorts and some pumps to exercise. Nowadays it's compulsory to pass the catwalk test before you're allowed in.

Anyway, going to a gym should really guarantee that I live forever. With the fees they charge I shan't be able to afford a funeral.

I've just completed my first circuit and I'm looking forward to being able to breathe again.

I said to one of the members, 'It'll be nice to get into the sauna to cool down a bit.'

There was a queue for the rowing machine but I didn't see anyone actually get away.

My wife paid for a one-hour trial. She had to book an extra hour to get her leotard off.

The instructor told her to always wear loose clothing. If she had loose clothing she wouldn't need the gym.

She became obsessed with one machine in the building. I'm sad to say it's the ATM.

Instructor: 'Do you do squats?'
    Member: 'No, I rent a small flat.'

Alton Douglas

GROUP THERAPY

That's My Business

Most of the time, as a comedian, I would work with singers, magicians or speciality acts but now and then it would be with a group. I thought it would be interesting to recall a few of those that I was on the bill with:

The Flowerpot Men, The Searchers, Helen Day and Catch, Joe Brown and the Bruvvers, The Black Abbots, The Kinks, The Hollies, The Rockin' Berries and The Temperance Seven (maybe not really known as a group - but there were a group of them!)

My week at The Shakespeare Theatre Club in Liverpool with The Flowerpot Men was enlivened even further by Paul McCartney and his then-girlfriend Jane Asher, coming backstage to say hello.

The Rockin' Berries were nearly all from Birmingham and their drummer, Keith Smart, was a neighbour.

The Temperance Seven topped the bill at Shanklin Pier Theatre (sadly no longer in existence) in the summer of 1972. I was the Principal Comic for thirteen weeks and what an experience that was! The famous 'man in the white suit' was replaced halfway through by Vivian Stanshall - the only genius I've ever met. To watch him entertain a party of handicapped children single-handed was something I shall remember for ever.

A riotous week was spent with Freddie and the Dreamers at the Cresta Club in Solihull. Freddie insisted on an offstage introduction. What the audience couldn't see was me attempting to be professional whilst he was trying to goose me. I'm sure my antics must have mirrored Freddie's onstage leaping about!

Alton Douglas

BOOK MARKS

That's My Business

Books have played such a major part in my life that I thought a few comments on them would not be out of place:

When I was very young my greatest ambition was to see my name in a book. How strange that now it's not only in books but on the spines of over sixty!

-.-.-.-

We humans are very perverse. In the most difficult of times in my life the one thing that has kept me sane is writing jokes. I started at around thirteen and, to this day, it is still my Number One occupation.

-.-.-.-

It was a book that led me to the best cup of coffee I have ever had.

In 1983 I interviewed the oldest living wartime Mayor, George Hodgkinson, for our book *Coventry at War*. His Scottish wife served me the most unforgettable nectar. I said to her, 'That is the best cup of coffee I have ever had - if I'm not being too intrusive do tell me the secret?' She smiled. 'Just a wee pinch of salt, Alton.'

To this day, despite numerous attempts, I have never recaptured that magic.

-.-.-.-

I am delighted to reveal that a couple of my friends, Pete Lindup and Keith Ackrill, have embarked on writing the stories of their lives and that wonderful magician, Leslie Melville, is still producing books. His most recent, *Peformance Storytelling,* is an absolute must for anyone reading stories for children.

Leslie included in his act a clairvoyant hen. I shall spend the rest of my life puzzling over that too. How did the chicken know which cards to choose?

Alton Douglas

HOSPITAL VISITS

That's My Business

In my band leading days I suddenly had a spate of nose bleeds. My doctor decided it would be best if the offending proboscis underwent cauterisation, so I found myself in hospital. On my first morning the hospital doctor on his rounds came towards me and I looked at his kindly face and his fine tapering fingers and I thought, 'I'm wasting my time in music - I should have gone in for something more worthwhile.' He stopped and said to me, 'I think you'll be discharged today. What is your occupation?' I mumbled, 'I play the trombone.' He took a slight step back and said, 'How I envy you musicians! We can only treat the physical person but you people reach their souls!'

-.-.-.-

For a few years Jo and I used to go in for hospital visiting on Christmas Day. We would try to visit all the patients who hadn't got a visitor and chat to them. However, one year, in the middle of a flu epidemic, we made our usual visit and afterwards developed the worst colds we had ever had. Sadly, call it cowardice if you like but that put paid to any future visiting.

-.-.-.-

I did a lot of theatre dates with Paul Daniels and quite often, after we had finished our band call, he would ask us to visit the local hospital with him. So, quite frequently, a surprised hospital staff would find a group of visiting vagabonds descending on them and doing impromptu bits and pieces to entertain their patients. I don't honestly know whether any of them had been pre-warned but it always seemed to go very well!

Alton Douglas

AROUND AND ABOUT

That's My Business

My neighbour is the only person I know who failed the speed awareness course.

He set out some time ago to be a baby doctor but he couldn't reach the table.

These days he works as a cosmetic surgeon with the motto 'See me if you need a lift'. A wag has chalked underneath 'If not, try a crane'.

I managed to see my doctor last week - from a distance but she did give me a wave.

It's a very quiet area, even the refuse collectors come round in carpet slippers.

I deny the rumour circulating that I tried to have the wife fitted with a silencer.

She says she wants to live somewhere green where the air is fresh. So far she's turned down my offer of a deckchair and a tent in the middle of a cabbage field.

The new traffic measures seem to be effective - it's the first time I've seen a policeman on point duty in a cul-de-sac.

There was consternation today when members of the senior citizens' club were fined for underage drinking.

Now the owner of the fish and chip shop has been arrested for battering his wife.
    (Prepare to duck) He said it was an Act of Cod.

Alton Douglas

SHARPEN YOUR CLAUSE

That's My Business

Some of the clauses included in film star's contracts may come as a surprise to you!

Margaret Rutherford: Every film she made had to include a role for her husband, Stringer Davis.

-.-.-.-

Roger Moore: In all seven of his Bond films he was entitled to an unlimited number of Montecristo cigars.

-.-.-.-

Queen Latifah: She insisted that she would never again be killed. (She said she had died publicly enough times already).

-.-.-.-

Samuel l. Jackson: His contract allowed for him to play golf twice every week.

-.-.-.-

Dolph Lundgren: The Swedish actor had so much trouble with his lines that his voice was often dubbed. He had a new clause inserted that said he would be given three attempts before any dubbing could take place.

-.-.-.-

Jack Nicholson: Extra time was allowed so that he could watch his favourite basketball team. When he filmed in England the matches were to be recorded, flown out to him and no one was allowed to discuss them until he had seen them.

Alton Douglas

COMEDY FROM HOME

That's My Business

Although Liverpool is considered by many to be the home of comedy, Birmingham produced at least a trio of comedians that any city can be proud of. Not comparing myself in any way with them, I can only speak from personal experience. I worked many weeks of cabaret in Liverpool and always received a good reception because, unlike most of their comics, who were all using the same material, I had my own self-penned gags. Anyway, I digress, this is not about me:

Sid Field: Born in Ladywood in 1904, the son of a candlemaker, at an early age he would charge his friends admission to see his comedy antics. He developed a mixture of jokes and impressions, which was quite unusual at that time, eventually 'discovering' the character for which he is best remembered, 'Slasher Green', the Cockney wide boy. He made several films, including *London Town*, *Cardboard Cavalier* and *Piccadilly Hayride*. He died in 1950.

-.-.-.-

Tony Hancock: He originated from Hall Green in 1924 but his family moved to Bournemouth three years later when his father became the manager of the Railway Hotel. After RAF service he decided that his forte was comedy and, as with Sid Field, it was a combination of gags and impressions. For seven years from 1951, he was a member of the radio programme *Educating Archie* and to this day, devoted fans of Tony can still quote chunks from his radio series *Hancock's Half Hour*. He also appeared in six films including *The Rebel* and *The Punch and Judy Man*. His statue stands in Old Square. He passed away in 1968.

-.-.-.-

Jasper Carrott: Born in Acocks Green in 1945, he began his working life in The Beehive, a large departmental store. In 1969 he started his own folk club, The Boggery, and his recording of *Funky Moped* proved very successful in the UK Hit Parade. Television appearances include the series *An Audience with Jasper Carrott* and *The Detectives*. Happily he is still with us!

Alton Douglas

THE OTHER HALF

That's My Business

In an act of defiance I said to my wife, 'When I need my opinion I'll ask you for it!'

She's not bad as far as wives go - unfortunately, she doesn't go far very often.

It was a very romantic proposal, all those years ago. I was blind drunk and she thought, 'At least it can't get any worse than this.'

The wedding went off quite well until it got to the bit when the vicar asked the big question and I blurted out, 'I suppose so if I must.'

I still think it's better than my Best Man. When the vicar asked him, he said, 'Can I phone a friend?'

I don't know how we finished up with so many children. I don't think I could have been concentrating.

I would never suggest that she's a nag but I've just discovered that she's been giving internet tutorials on the subject.

She had her first driving lesson last Tuesday. On Wednesday the instructor signed on at the Job Centre.

Still, we mustn't complain about her - I suppose you can do but it's at your peril.

I don't think she's ever been unfaithful to me but, now that we're older, sometime I must ask her about all those notches on her walking stick.

A friend told me that she had a face like the back of a bus. I was indignant, 'How dare you! I've always thought it was more like the front!'

Alton Douglas

ODD IT IS

That's My Business

One of my dearest friends was the late Pat Astley. Pat had been a continuity announcer for ATV in the 1960s and '70s and a presenter of the children's programme *The Tingha and Tucker Club* and we recorded several radio commercials together.
   In his back garden was a Union flag on top of an enormous flagpole. 'That flag does not come down till our lads return from the Falklands,' he told me. He had created in his back bedroom a model of a World War II German fuel dump that he had been involved in blowing up, miles behind the enemy lines. He could be seen sitting in a jeep, with such minute details, even to the perspiration on his shirt.

-.-.-.-

I was sorry to hear that Chaim Topol had passed away in 2023. Jo and I saw him three times in the West End, with his magnificent portrayal of Tevye in *Fiddler On The Roof*, and in the late '60s I used to do an impression of him in my act. My involvement didn't end there because he had his own production company and in 1988 I was the archives and stills consultant for his programme *Made In Birmingham*.

-.-.-.-

Not a Showbiz story but I can't wait to tell you this:
   Problems with our main drain meant quite extensive work for a two-man team. They performed admirably and, at the end, the older man, who had been up to his chest digging up roots, clambered out and with an obvious show of satisfaction filled it all in and cemented over. Time to go home and I saw a look of panic on his face. 'Where the f--- are my keys?' You're ahead of me! The hole had to be re-dug and at the very bottom were the missing keys. Back went the debris, on with the cement, and the job done. I was as relieved as him until he stopped in his tracks and I heard, 'Where the f--- is my phone?'

Alton Douglas

SIGNS OF THE TIMES

That's My Business

I have enjoyed notices and signs all my life. These are a few that I've actually seen - or are some of them the products of an over-active imagination?

'Nurses should remove their uniforms before appearing in public places such as shops.'

'Stylish hairdressing while you wait.'

'If you have any trouble with your hearing we would like to speak to you.'

'Push this door unless you are on the other side.'

'Beware of the bull. He doesn't distinguish between friend and foe.'

'Danger deep excavations - see below.'

'Staff Room for the use of staff.'

'If the Fire Alarm sounds exit the building as quickly as possible.' (No - I think I'll stop and make a sandwich!)

(This was on a Waiting Room wall) 'Do not pull the chain whilst the train is in the station.'

'Hard hats should be worn wherever this sign is displayed.'

'Please switch off when not in use, otherwise leave on.'

'Eye protection must be worn with safety boots.'

'The use of mobile phones is prohibited. Call Head Office to report offenders.'

'The mailbox is temporarily out of use. Further information will be posted.'

Alton Douglas

'CCTV to help us identify persons selling drugs.'

'Caution: men may be working.'

'This exit is not an entrance'

'Please return your plates and cutlery for washing.'

'Flytipping is a crime.' (The local wag had contributed, 'But flies work SO hard.')

'Complaints Dept open on odd days.'

'Your call is very important to us. Do not phone between the hours of 1 and 2.'

A board outside a church proclaimed, 'God sees everything.' On a smaller board next to it, 'Please report any suspicious activity.'

'Long distance lorry drivers required. Must be prepared to travel.'

'In the interests of hygiene, wash both hands.'

'In the case of an emergency, please send the details in triplicate to the address listed below.'

'Nude sunbathing is allowed in this area. The use of telescopes is strictly prohibited.'

'Open seven days a week including Sunday.'

'To turn right keep to the left.'

'Guard dogs are permanently on petrol.'

'This floor's past inspection.'

'To operate the automatic door, press the button on the side.'

That's My Business

'Always keep two meters apart.'

'Our flashlights are for use in the dark.'

'To gain access, press the bell if it's working.'

'No bad language will be tolerated towards members of staff and that includes the Manager.'

Alton Douglas

OUR FOREIGN FRIENDS

That's My Business

We are a motley crew in Showbiz! The great thing is that it is made up not only of people with differing ways and temperaments but also with different nationalities:

The Band of the 5th Royal Inniskilling Dragoon Guards played at all manner of functions and one of them was in Germany in Brackweder at a 1957 Schutzenfest. - that's an annual fair or festival. There we were, not more than a dozen years after the end of the Second World War, being accepted and feted by the Germans - something that amazed me because everyone was so friendly. In the evenings we were let loose and, you might guess, decided to play again. We joined forces (excuse the pun) and played at a free-for-all concert with musicians from both nationalities. However, Anglo-German relationships were not improved, judging by the looks in my direction from one of their trombonists!

-.-.-.-

Being a jazz lover I was thrilled to be booked with the brilliant Dutch guitarist Wout Steenhuis for a gig in Cambridgeshire. I knew of his background with the Dutch Swing College Orchestra, one of my favourite jazz bands, and so I couldn't wait to meet him. He turned out to be extremely friendly and we got on very well. Everything was fine until it came to the work! It transpired that he had to play and I had to do a 40 minute comedy act in a vast circus tent. Poor Wout fared as badly.

-.-.-.-

I have mentioned before my admiration for Stephane Grappelli and the fact that I worked with him on several occasions. However, I was greatly saddened to see him, towards the end of his life, being pushed around in the daytime in a wheelchair by one of his fellow musicians. By the evening he performed on stage transformed, for the time, like a much younger Stephane. Showbiz can have a magical effect on all of us!

Alton Douglas

BEDSIDE MANOR

That's My Business

How many doctors does it take to change a light bulb? Two. One to shake his head and the other one to say, 'I told you it was dead!'

'Doctor, I keep thinking that I'm the elephant in the room.'
   'I'm sorry but we don't discuss that.'

'My wife's livid because I keep seeing things.'
   'That doesn't seem fair.'
   'I know, I've told her that.'
   'What do you keep seeing?'
   'Other women.'

Our doctor's been prescribed a cure for nervous exhaustion - take one patient a day.

He should have been given at least a week off but he couldn't get a sick note.

I don't think that receptionist is going to be around for long. I said, 'Can I see the doctor, please?' She said, 'Over my dead body!'

'Doctor, why do you only see patients in your lunch hour?'
   'I'm on a diet.'

He told me I need to keep fit. 'Run a mile and report to me in the morning.' I said, 'What, from that distance?'

I was prescribed some sleeping tablets. By the time I'd opened the bottle it was morning.

My sister is absent minded. She was given the morning-after pills but could never remember the night before.

Alton Douglas

DRAGGING AROUND

That's My Business

I played Dame in pantomime on a couple of occasions, both at the White Rock Pavilion in Hastings. 1969 was a sheer delight as Mrs Crusoe, replete with cocoa tin lids as buttons, Afro hair one minute and a frizzy perm the next, badly-played banjo the next - the knockabout part was great fun. However, the following year I was back as Queen Wilhelmina in *Puss in Boots*, with gorgeous dresses and beautiful wigs and I hated every second of it.

Over the years I have to admit that, with one exception, I couldn't enjoy drag acts - too blue for my fragile ears. I was lucky in that I was only ever booked with a few.

My mother was far from prim and so I took a chance and she came with me to a nearby working men's club. It was literally only round the corner and she had never been to one before and was curious to see the kind of venues I was working at that early stage in my career. The sad misfortune was that the other act was The Dolly Sisters. Mum was flabbergasted at the type of material and some of the language. As I've said she was far from narrow minded but this was something else. One of them saw this dumbfounded-looking woman and shouted out to her, 'If you don't start laughing I'll come over there and ---- in your handbag!'

-.-.-.-

The only drag act I did like to be on the same bill with was Adrian Varcoe. Whenever we did a show together, his Mum would be with him to act as his dresser and it meant a laughter-filled night for all three of us. If I appeared anywhere in Bristol, his beloved home town, he would somehow find out and bring a large party of friends to cheer me on. When the local branch of Equity held their annual dinner Adrian insisted they book me as the cabaret - what a wonderful night that was! Sadly, Adrian and his mother are no longer with us but I can still hear the laughter.

Alton Douglas

PETTY CHAT

That's My Business

When I was young we had a family living near to us that kept every type of pet imaginable - their conversations I COULD imagine:

'I can't understand it? That parrot's language is as bad as mine!'

'What do you want to keep a snake for? If you want something that's non-communicative, non-tactile and totally lacking in affection, there's always your Uncle Fred.'

'His missus is like a tortoise - in bed all day and only sticks her head out to eat.'

'Ignorant! That lad was convinced that thing was only a mouse until it gnawed its way through the iron leg of our kitchen table.'

'There are that many pets in this house I think it must be raining cats and dogs.'

'I've just made a cat flap. I threatened it with the vet.'

'That ex-police dog you bought - I took it in the car and it bit me for not wearing a seat belt.'

'You'll have to get rid of that dog. Every time it comes back from The Poodle Parlour your mother gets jealous.'

'Don't bother buying any more rabbits - they're quite capable of doing their own shopping.'

'I've just bought you all an aquarium. I thought it would be nice for the fish to see nothing happening all day.'

'What's the point of keeping goldfish? You won't remember to feed them and they won't remember to remind you.'

Alton Douglas

'FOR YOU THE WAR IS OVER'

That's My Business

I was amazed to discover how many actors were prisoners of war - here some examples:

FIRST WORLD WAR

Maurice Chevalier: During his French National Service he was captured and spent two years in a German camp. It was there that he learned to speak English.

-.-.-.-

Ronald Adam: Shot down by The Red Baron (Manfred von Richthofen) he spent a year and a half in captivity.

-.-.-.-

SECOND WORLD WAR

Donald Pleasance: Serving as a wireless operator his plane was shot down in 1944. In 1963 he played the forger in *The Great Escape*.

-.-.-.-

Sam Kydd: He spent five years as a prisoner. After three years he refused repatriation in order to continue running the camp's theatrical activities. He told of his time there in his book *For You The War Is Over*.

-.-.-.-

Peter Butterworth: A lieutenant in the Fleet Air Arm, during his time behind the wire he became one of the vaulters covering for the escapers which was later shown in the film *The Wooden Horse*. In 1949 he auditioned for the film but was told he did not look heroic enough!

-.-.-.-

Percy Herbert: Captured at the fall of Singapore in 1942, he was held at the notorious Changi Japanese prison and forced to work on the Burma Railway.

Alton Douglas

Derek Bond: Awarded the Military Cross whilst in the 3rd Grenadiers, he was later caught and held in a Bavarian camp.

-.-.-.-

Denholm Elliott: Taking part in an air raid on U-Boats in 1942, he finished up in the North Sea, was picked up and imprisoned for the rest of the war. He formed a theatrical group and toured several other camps performing *Twelfth Night*.

-.-.-.-

Michael Goodliffe: He was one of the many caught in Dunkirk in 1940. His obituary mistakenly was published but he did, in fact, live until his suicide in 1976.

-.-.-.-

Roy Dotrice: After the plane crashed in which he was a rear gunner, he was a prisoner with all seven of his fellow crew members for four years.

-.-.-.-

Desmond Llewelyn: Captured in France he was held in the notorious Colditz Castle for five years.

That's My Business

There were many Americans who were POWs but perhaps I'll leave their stories to other authors. Just a final thought on the subject - there are unexpected twists in the course of a war and I found this tale particularly intriguing:

Hardy Kruger: At 16 he was drafted into the 38th SS Nibelungen. Ordered to shoot at an American squad, he refused and was sentenced to death for cowardice. He was kept in prison for a short while but an SS Officer countermanded the order and he was released. He escaped from Germany and hid in Tyrol until the end of the war. He always said that the experience caused him to break completely with Nazism.

Alton Douglas

DIGGING IN

That's My Business

Sitting in the digs, listening to my fellow club acts provided a rich supply of material:

'Someone said they do have a sense of humour in the North East. The trouble is that one isn't much between all of them.'

'Talk about dying a death. I think that last night I attended my own funeral.'

'I should take your own backing tapes there. The band can not only not read music but they've barely conquered the concept of speech.'

'As a girl singer I'd advise you to take your own sound system too - unless you want to sound like Louis Armstrong on speed.'

'That was the noisiest club I've ever worked in. Fortunately the compere was a bookie so he introduced me using Tic-Tac.'

'Halfway through the evening it all really kicked off. Rough! There was a police raid and nobody noticed.'

'I'd stopped a policeman to ask him the best way to get to the club. He shook his head, "I'd say, if I were you, wearing a blindfold and ear plugs."

'I still had a terrible game finding the place - unfortunately I did.'

'That's the last time I work with a drag act. Without much effort he was prettier than me!'

'The price of booze these days I think I might have to start doing my act sober.'

'That double act! Neither of them was as funny as the other one thought he was.'

Alton Douglas

GETTING IT OFF MY CHEST

That's My Business

The female form seems to figure (excuse the pun) in some of my memories so perhaps it would be best to get a trio of them off my chest:

When I was quite small Mum would send me on errands but only as far as the little sweet shop about 200 yards from where we lived in Heather Road in Small Heath. I suspect now it may have been to hear my response. The shop was owned by two women of strikingly contrasting appearances. Mum would say, 'Who served you today then?' and my reply would inevitably be, 'The one with the chesses.'

-.-.-.

It must have been about that time that I overheard a conversation between Mum and my aunty. 'Ivy, don't you think you ought to do something about your figure?' Indignantly the reply was, 'Well, I'm sorry if it offends you, Dolly, but I'm not one of these young girls that can throw 'em over my shoulders!'

-.-.-.-

I played Mrs Crusoe, in *Robinson Crusoe* at the White Rock Pavilion in Hastings in 1969. The producer Audrey Maye said to me, after one performance, 'Alton, what happened to your figure in the second half? You had your usual padded bra on in the first half and then all of a sudden you were totally flat chested!' I was very apologetic. 'I'm sorry, Audrey, I really didn't think anyone would notice but you've given me such a large chest that it gets in the way every night when I play the trombone.'

Incidentally, the Dame is normally played by a much older comic so, as far as I can trace, I must have been at 31 one of the youngest to fill the role. I must have got something right because the next year I was back again as Queen Wilhelmina in *Puss in Boots*!

Alton Douglas

SOME YOU LOSE

That's My Business

Sometimes even the best of acts can find themselves in trouble - anything from a misplaced gag, a misplaced spot on the bill or a misplaced spot on the premises. Any artiste that tells you that they have always sailed trouble free through their careers is either lying or suffering from terrible memory loss!

March 1968 found me on a bill for a week at the Ace of Clubs in Worksop with Josef Locke as the top of the bill. The other comedian on the opening night was Jackie Carlton. Sadly, that's all Jackie lasted. He spotted a Sikh, complete with turban, in the audience and chose to say, 'Hope your head gets better, mate.' The man he picked on was a local war hero. Jackie was ushered off the premises.

-.-.-.-

I was booked for the second year running for an annual function at Llanidloes Community Centre. Sid Francis, the comedian and trumpet player, always a strong act, unfortunately was placed in the running order immediately after comedy magician, Denis Beards. Anyone who has worked with Denis would know that that was not an ideal spot! His zany comedy never failed to convulse audiences, and this night was no exception. Poor Sid struggled and hopelessly failed. The organiser refused to pay him and Sid was so livid that when he got into the car he snatched his toupee off and threw it at the windscreen.

-.-.-.-

One of my engagements was for four nights at a nightclub in the heart of Wales. On a boiling hot summer's night I was parched and went downstairs to see if I could get a soft drink. By this time the club was closed and in the dark I tripped over a couple of bodies grappling in the corridor. I mumbled my apologies and scuttled back to my room. I had no idea who the pair were but guessed they were of mixed gender. The next morning a red-faced owner called me into his office and told me my services would no longer be required.

Alton Douglas

OUT OF MY MIND

That's My Business

I'm in the middle of writing my next novel. When I say in the middle, I've just bought a pencil sharpener.

People ask me, 'Why don't you use a computer?' The last time I saw mine it was in mid-air on its way through the lounge window.

Every time I come up with a good plot I find somebody like Charles Dickens has cribbed the idea.

It's a murder mystery but the plot is a bit involved - I've no idea who the murderer is. I may have to leave it to the detective in charge to sort it out.

The publisher says if it makes as much in royalties as my last book it should make quite a sizeable hole in my finances.

He doesn't seem to be over confidant - he's having it printed on non-retardant paper.

The title is a choice between Dead on Arrival and Guess What the Postman's Brought Today.

The villain is a dog-faced man with an outdoor occupation and a guttural accent - he's a German Shepherd.

The suggested blurb for the back cover is 'As murder mysteries go it's clueless.'

I thought I'd try a bit of pre-selling so I went in and mentioned it to our local librarian. They reckon she'll be able to work again sometime in the future.

Alton Douglas

NOW YOU ALMOST SEE THEM ----

That's My Business

Over the years I auditioned for many different jobs. I suppose the ratio for success/failure would be about 50/50. Amongst those in the first category I would include being signed up by Astor Productions (they owned London's Astor Club), ATV's *Muck and Brass* and the role of Dame in Bunny Baron's *Robinson Crusoe* at the White Rock Pavilion in Hastings, and the failures would include a season in New Brighton and a role in the film *Prostitute*! There were also auditions that were carried out by what I would term the 'Often Invisibles'. These were people who sneaked in to see me, obviously were not too impressed and sneaked out again without so much as a by-your-leave.

Richard Stone, who managed such diverse artistes as Barbara Windsor, Benny Hill, Ian Carmichael, Bill Owen, Victoria Wood and Bill Maynard, was recommended to see me by the latter. He did come to see our summer show in Blackpool but that was that - not a word.

-.-.-.-

Harry Secombe's manager, Jimmy Grafton, heard about my success at the Best Cellar in Leicester Square and was involved in the casting of *The Four Musketeers* at the Theatre Royal in Drury Lane. He came to see me but all I saw of him was his backside as he retreated up the stairs and out of the nightclub. I didn't even make it as the Fifth Musketeer!

-.-.-.-

Our friend, multi-instrumentalist Linda Grant, recommended me to Esther Rantzen. She was looking for a replacement presenter for her *That's Life* television series. I sent them a list of my bookings for the following week and was told that someone would come to see my act at a very nice venue in Sutton Coldfield. The show went extremely well, I never spoke to anyone afterwards but assumed they would go back to London, report in and a decision would be made.

I did hear a few days later to say that their 'scout' had turned up the following Saturday only to find he'd missed me by seven days. I gave them alternative dates but never heard another word.

Alton Douglas

WHAT'S IN A NAME?

That's My Business

Prime embarrassment! My friend Dennis Moore, an ex-RAF Officer and, as a manager at a Black Country bank, a dignified and highly respected member of the community. He puts a Monty Python television programme on and hears 'Dennis Moore, Dennis Moore, riding through the glen' (à la Robin Hood theme).

-.-.-.-.-

You may have difficulty in believing it but these are actual names of American politicians:
   Newt Gingrich
   Zephyr Teachout
   Krystal Ball
   Kinky Friedman
   Frank Schmuck
   And the best we can offer? Crispin Blunt.

-.-.-.-

Nobody believes me when I tell them that my brother actually went out with a girl named Felicity Punter.

That, in turn, inspired a verse that I included in my children's book *A Load of Nonsense* in 2006. (It works well if you sing it.)

>   Felicity Punter and Peregrine Gunter
>   And Hilary Willoughby-Smythe,
>   Philately Battersea (even Roy Hattersley)
>   Gilda Matilda (nee Blythe).
>   Percy Pirantha and Charlie Chrysanthe-
>   Mum, Boris Zee, Morrisey James,
>   Henrietta Baretta, Loretta Coletta
>   Are thinking of changing their names.

(Reprinted by kind permission of Brewin Books Ltd.)

Alton Douglas

*SCUTTLEBUTT CORNER

That's My Business

The news reports seem to become more bizarre and gossip-like with every passing day and you think to yourself, 'You couldn't make it up!'

'China has announced that there is still an untethered male bovine animal in the commercial premises.'

'Clock and watch manufacturers throughout the country will be going on strike today - at precisely 11am.'

'Due to the shortage of hospital beds a new system of patient sharing is to be instigated called, "Two for the space of one." '

'The CWU (Communication Workers Union) is demanding an extra payment for all postmen who have to walk to work.'

'Car Parks are such an expensive luxury these days it's cheaper to just keep driving.'

'Time for our weather report now - or as we call it the "Grab-a-pin-close-your-eyes-and-hope-for-the-best forecast."'

'More trade union problems as Unite say that crane drivers are very unhappy with what they pick up.'

'Pensioners are revolting.'

'Following the sudden increase in global warming the Green Party will now be known as "The Green and Somewhat Brown Party." '

'The General Election will be held next Thursday. The results will be announced later today.'

'The BBC has stated that it will definitely be increasing the licence fee later this year, in line with inclination.'

*Scuttlebutt is thought of, these days, as a Naval term but in slang it means gossip or rumour.

Alton Douglas

'The firm, specialising in miniature offices, has said that the new Government regulations are cramping their style.'

'As the cost of electricity continues to escalate the Blackpool Corporation has announced that, this year, the entire Illumination display will be dedicated to the Wartime blackout.'

'Herr Kutts has decided to extend his hairdressing empire as far as the Barbary Coast.'

'Teachers throughout the UK say the new terms they have been offered are 'unmigitated ecksploitashion.''

'NHS junior doctors maintain that they are old enough and mature enough to get the same pay as senior doctors. They say that if it's not forthcoming they won't ever play *Doctors and Nurses* anymore.'

'The ferry operator has decided to retire as the job is too confusing. He can never make up his mind if he's coming or going.'

'The firm, who make loyalty cards, have said that all their regular customers are going elsewhere.'

'Later today the police will be looking into the broken church window and the vicar says they will be seeing the verger.'

'The Flat Earth Society tells us that a significant number of new members have been dropping off recently.'

'The lady who complained about the result of her Botox injections has been told to face facts and develop a stiff upper lip.'

'The Potholing Society of Great Britain has complained bitterly about the council filling in so many potholes.'

'

That's My Business

'With a failed romance behind him he wanted to forget - so he ran away to join the British Legion.'

'Councils throughout the UK have noticed that so many cars are being parked on pavements that a change in the law is necessary. From the first of next month it will be mandatory for all pedestrians to walk down the middle of the road.'

'Nudist's demonstration to get full coverage.'

'Today, for the first time, several members of His Majesty's Government have been accused of selling secrets to an enemy state. Yesterday, Russia denied any knowledge of such activity.'

A true story: A friend of mine is an excellent photographer. He posted a selection of his pictures on the internet but discovered the following day that several of them had been deleted. On enquiring he was informed, 'All pictures of people with thin legs have been removed. There are so many sites encouraging anorexic behaviour that we thought it best.' You could not make it up!

Alton Douglas

TIME FOR THE TOAST

That's My Business

Some of our acquisitions! I arrived at a hotel in Northampton to speak at a dinner. The Toastmaster was my friend Jack Ablett. He had with him a huge front-of-house b/w photo of Max Miller. I said, 'That would be perfect on my wall!' Jack said, 'I've actually promised it to the hotelier but would you like it?' Guess my answer. He said, 'Nip out round to that window. and I'll pass it through.' The framed picture nestled in my car boot and now adorns my front room wall.

-.-.-.-

The Principal Girl in *Robinson Crusoe* at the White Rock Pavilion in Hastings in 1969 - in which I was the Dame - was Vanessa Kind. Her father Ken was not only a Toastmaster but also an agent. Our meeting resulted in my being booked by him for several years afterwards and culminated in my being chosen as the cabaret act for the London Guild of Toastmasters' annual dinner one year - from that came a lot more work in the south of England.

-.-.-.

On page 19 in *Funny's the Word* you will read of my solitary bad experience with a Toastmaster. What I didn't mention was his physique. Bear in mind that most TMs fulfilled the traditional image of a huge, barrel-chested Sergeant Major shape with a voice that could rock Big Ben. This particular character, who vocally was the equal of any of them, was only about 5'3". When he stood at the top table to make his announcements even at full stretch he was only the same height as his seated audience. The result was that the entire audience were convinced that the Invisible Man was responsible.

Alton Douglas

THE ODDS ON MY CITY

That's My Business

In Birmingham there is a narrow way off Bull Street and opposite where Grey's used to be sited, which leads to the Friends Meeting House. Surely someone in the council could have come up with a better name than Dr Johnson's Passage!

-.-.-.-

On the other hand it could be considered quite appropriate that the street where George Bartram's publicity office was situated should be called Gas Street.

-.-.-.-

The oldest working cinema in the country is the Electric Cinema in Station Street, built in 1909.

-.-.-.-

It is claimed, and just as often disputed, that Birmingham has more miles of canals than Venice. Let's just satisfy ourselves that 35 miles of canals is a lot of canals.

-.-.-.-

Here's something I bet you didn't know - there is a crater on the Moon called 'Birmingham'!

-.-.-.-

JR Tolkien used names of places and people in *The Hobbit* and *Lord of the Rings* drawn from the area where he lived in Moseley.

Alton Douglas

BEING A SPORT

That's My Business

Brian Close, the captain of the Somerset county team, was a very good friend of ex-Black and White Minstrel star Tony Mercer so he brought the entire team to see our show *Summer Showboat* at the Knightstone Theatre in Weston-Super-Mare during the summer of 1970. Afterwards he asked me if I would appear later in the year in his Testimonial show at the Wakefield Theatre Club. I said I would.

I thought no more about it until in the middle of a week in Wales for the agent Chris Banks, I received a call from a very excited Chris. 'I can't believe it but I've just heard from BRIAN CLOSE! He played for England! He asked me if I would release you on Wednesday night to take part in his show – how could I even think of saying "No" to HIM!'

I did the show, along with Tony, and Brian treated me to a super meal and presented me with a Yorkshire club tie.

-.-.-.-

I arrived at a club in the Black Country (don't ask where or when - I can't remember) to find comedian Tony Kent, already there - we had been double booked! I decided that as he had travelled all the way down from the North it should be his night. I missed my fee but cemented a friendship that survives to this day.

Over the years we worked together several times and both of us even appeared in straight parts in the TV drama series *Muck and Brass*. My joke has been, since then, that I always got the muck and Tony got the brass.

Alton Douglas

CAMPING OUT

That's My Business

I have no complaints about our treatment at the Derbyshire Miners Welfare Holiday Centre in Skegness in 1967, but other people haven't always had the greatest experience at different camps:

I'd been there four days before I discovered that the loudspeaker announcements were not in German.

The accommodation is on the cramped side. The chalet maid reckons that she can make our beds and the people's next door at the same time.

At mealtimes always try to be on the first sitting - that way you should avoid leftovers.

The food isn't exactly ideal - today's Queen of Puddings was more Victoria than Elizabeth.

I don't think the man in charge of the children's entertainment had got much idea. In the kids' egg and spoon race he won.

The frontline staff double as entertainers. After seeing their first show I'm not entirely convinced that 1 for 2 is always such a good idea.

It was a bit embarrassing when the knobbly knees competition was won by the Head Girl.

The other girls call her 'Blondi'. Not because of her hair colour but her resemblance to Hitler's dog.

I think the Entertainment Manager is a bit over-ambitious in his choice of films for the camp cinema. Other camps get *Carry On*-type entertainment and he's chosen a season of Swedish art films.

The security men come round at 10 o'clock to check if the single guests have anyone in their room that shouldn't be there. Do you think, if you haven't, they'd supply one?

Alton Douglas

MAKING ME REDUNDANT

That's My Business

Sometimes, when I see how the world is developing, I think that writers like me will soon no longer be required. Even discounting AI (artificial intelligence) we just couldn't create events as odd or as unbelievable as life itself comes up with:

One of the conditions for joining the artistes' trade union, Equity, was that you had to produce a contract to prove you were a working pro. No one explained how you could get a decent booking without first being a member of Equity.

-.-.-.-

Last year I decided it was about time that I treated myself to some new handkerchiefs. Off I went to M & S in Longbridge, expecting to find them in the Men's Department. After a fruitless search and joined by three assistants we were on the point of giving up when we spotted them. How foolish of us not to look there first! There they were, beautifully displayed on a pristine stand - in the Furniture Department!

-.-.-.-

A few years ago an excellent job was done of re-laying the pavement outside our row of houses. The following week it was all dug up again to allow for new cables to be put down. The workmen told us that the council knew well in advance but still went ahead with the original work. Excuse me?

-.-.-.-

Once, having been on blood pressure tablets for a number of years, the medication was changed. A fortnight later, as normal with changes, I had a blood test. Four days later the phone rang. 'Mr Douglas, it's the surgery here. You weren't checked for cholesterol, could you come back for another test, please.' A few days on, 'Sorry about this but your PSA should have been included.' Back I went, for the third time, safe in the knowledge that that would be it. The phone rang a week later. 'Mr Douglas, it's the surgery here - it's time to book you in for your annual blood test.'

Alton Douglas

READ ALL ABOUT IT!

That's My Business

As those of you who have read *I Look At It Like This* will know, I wrote a fortnightly column for a Midlands newspaper in the 1970s. These are a few excerpts I thought you might find of interest:

Tailor Made

Right in the heart of Stirchley in Birmingham is one of the most prestigious shops in the country - 'Wilton Pugh - the Aristocrat of Menswear'. Apart from their 'normal' clients the shop has built up a great reputation among the Showbiz community and artistes travel from all over the country to buy stagewear.

Peter Gordeno, David Whitfield, Frank Ifield, Don Maclean and even yours truly are seen on stage dressed by Wilton Pugh. But apart from clothing Mr Pugh keeps one other unusual commodity in stock - Mrs Pugh!

For tucked away amongst the suits stirs a tailor-made singer. Starting with the Three Jays and then the Two Jays she now works as the one Jay. Or rather she did until she saw that Jillian had been printed as Julian on a club poster and she thought it best to become Gillian Pugh.

-.-.-.-

Magical

Our magical celebrity from Kings Norton, Mike Gancia is once again in the news. He's just been made a member of the Magic Circle with Gold Star. We travelled together to Portland Bill (that's a place, not a local character) last week and got caught up in the most awful fog. With visibility as bad as that, the audience couldn't see my jokes or Mike's tricks!

I got a great thrill out of the recent unveiling of the Tony Hancock plaque in Southam Road in Birmingham. Along with quite a few other people I had agitated for some kind of memorial to the lad from 23 Railway Cuttings.

Alton Douglas

Doddy's Wordsmith

Last year one of Ken Dodd's scriptwriters, Maurice Bird, decided to set out on a journey from Land's End to John O'Groats to raise money for kidney patients. The story of his exploits has been published in paperback under the title *The Toss of a Coin*. It recounts the hilarious and often dramatic adventures that befell an over-weight and, by his own admission, slightly unfit character, precariously balanced on a bicycle. Maurice asked me to pen an introduction to his escapades and I told him, 'I'll do anything to help as long as I don't have to pedal as well!' I'd be about as gainly as Cyril Smith in a ballet skirt.

-.-.-.-

Alton's Travels

I've been back on the road again this month in hot pursuit of an audience. Sunday found me at Weymouth Pavilion in the good company of the Dallas Boys, Julie Rogers with her husband ex-big bandleader Teddy Foster (who, sad to say, is not playing trumpet very often these days) and Alan Randall.

Alan, an old friend from Nuneaton, has a new LP out called *The Alan Randall Souvenir Album* and on it he demonstrates, as he does in his stage act, that the George Formby impression is only a small part of his talent. Apart from re-vamping some of the old Formby numbers, on Side 2 he shows how well he can play the vibes. I think it's such a pity that the general public only think of Alan with the ukelele and the toothy grin when in fact he plays a lot of instruments extremely well.

On Wednesday I was back to my Fol-de-Rols stamping ground, Bexhill, for an Olde Tyme Music Hall, at the De La Warr Pavilion. It's amazing how a few old songs (and gags to match) can pull the crowds in!

The following weekend I was in Bolton and then on to Newquay Dyfed once more. The enterprising Holimarine management have taken the trouble to record a brief excerpt from some of this summer's artistes (with their permission, of course) and now they've just released a record.

That's My Business

Music Par Excellence

Dave Brubeck came to the BBC studios last Monday to record an hour of music and what an event it was! With his son Chris on bass, ex-Basie drummer Butch Miles and tenorist Gerry Bergonzi, the white-haired maestro rocked the building to its foundations.

During one riotous up tempo number a technical fault developed and the quartet had to repeat the same basic tune again. That's when jazz really excels!

-.-.-.-

Taking Vera's Place!

A hurried call from Lawrence Banner had me scurrying across to the Stathallan Hotel. Due to a mix up with dates the Warley branch of the British Empire Cancer Campaign for Research discovered that Vera Lynn would not be in Birmingham for another couple of days. As they'd asked her to accept a cheque on behalf of research for £3,000 you can imagine the consternation that reigned! So, an hour after my last appearance on BBC One's *Know your Place*, I found myself there expecting to find a bitterly disappointed audience. Instead, however, I discovered that the whole hotel was anxious to discuss the exciting final that I had just presided over!

For those who weren't able to see the end of our series, Hereford emerged as the triumphant victors. One or two of our competitors have blossomed out into real television personalities. I understand that Peter Hill, who is currently playing King Arthur in *Camelot* at Hereford's Nell Gwynne Theatre is now greatly in demand as an after-dinner speaker!

Alton Douglas

BIG BAND BLUES

That's My Business

I was a great fan of Eric Delaney's drumming and so Jo and I booked to see his orchestra at Birmingham Town Hall in the mid 1960s. The only tickets we could get placed us actually on the stage immediately behind the band. Unfortunately, just a few bars of his tympani playing and the stage reverberated and the effect on my stomach necessitated a very hasty exit!

-.-.-.-

The Tommy Dorsey Orchestra, led by Sam Donahue, at the Odeon in Birmingham, was a big attraction for me. I thoroughly enjoyed the evening but the only snag was the adenoidal singing of Frank Sinatra Junior. Some people don't seem able to resist the temptation to cash in on the family name.

-.-.-.-

Beacon Radio sponsored Herb Miller and the Glenn Miller Orchestra at Dudley Town Hall in the mid 1980s. As I had my own big band programme every Wednesday night on their station, I went along to represent them. In our conversation after the show, to my disappointment Herb came across as quite bitter about his brother and not in the least bit grateful for the fact that Glenn had given him a living for several years.

-.-.-.-

My only experience of playing in a big band was with the dance band of the 5th Royal Inniskilling Dragoon Guards when the bandleader, Sgt Mick Clifford, strictly forbade me to take any trombone solos!

-.-.-.-

My great ambition, as a lad, was to lead my own big band. The nearest I ever got to that was a quartet!

Alton Douglas

RIPPLES IN PARADISE

That's My Business

As I've mentioned before, Showbiz isn't always a sea of calm waters:

I spent two very lengthy summer seasons in revues at the South Shore Casino, in Blackpool, in 1969 and 1971 (I was offered a third, in 1973, but had to turn it down because I was so heavily involved in television warm-ups.) Although I was top of the bill for both seasons, I suggested to the producer, Bettina Merson, that, for the '69 show, with me and two singers it would be better, for the balance of the show, if I went on in the middle - she agreed. All went well until, halfway through the run, Rafael Lamas stepped forward in the finale and took a solo bow. I said to him afterwards, 'Look, you are not top of the bill - you only go on at the end because I've suggested it would make a better programme - please don't do it again because you insult Jill Rogers, the dancers and me by doing that.' He nodded but the next night did exactly the same thing. I stormed into his dressing room, 'Raf, I've asked you not to do that. If you do it tomorrow night I will kick your backside so hard you'll finish up in the balcony!' He never did do it again but neither did he ever speak to me again.

Incidentally, the seasons at the Casino, at 32 weeks, were the longest summer shows in the country. We used to finish up in what seemed like the depths of winter!

-.-.-.-

I was quite friendly with one of the security men in the resort and used to stop most nights, on my way in, to chat to him. One night he said to me, 'Come over here, Alton, I've got a present for you.' He chose a secluded spot, opened a case he'd kept hidden and opened it to reveal what looked like almost every type of forbidden drug created. 'Help yourself, mate.' I was flabbergasted. 'I'm sorry but I don't drink or smoke and wouldn't dream of taking drugs.' He shrugged and muttered, 'Please yourself, I just wanted to give you something.' A few weeks later, not in any way connected with me, he was arrested.

On reflection I realised that, although it was misguided, he just thought he was being kind!

Alton Douglas

EXCUSE ME

That's My Business

For various reasons, over the years, I must have heard a great many excuses, for different reasons, but only a few have remained with me:

Drop in to see any artiste, even the closest of friends, and if you congratulated them on their act they would always say the same thing, no matter how well they had gone, 'They weren't too bad tonight but you should have been in last night - wow!'

-.-.-.-

I have never really minded when other acts have used my original material (I suppose I've been flattered) as long as it wasn't on the same bill. When I chastised a comic on the bill with me that night for doing just that, he said, 'Oh, I didn't think you'd mind - you seem such a nice chap.'

-.-.-.-

Alec Fyne, the Head of Light Entertainment at ATV, rang me after I had replaced Norman Vaughan that Sunday, on *The Golden Shot*. He was glowing in his praise but I couldn't resist saying to him, 'I really appreciate you ringing, Mr Fyne, but would it not be possible to consider me for something other than being a warm-up comic?' He sounded stunned at my effrontery but then, after a lengthy pause said, 'But, Alton, being a warm-up comic is a highly specialised job - who would we get to take your place?' I replied, 'There are lots of comics out there in Clubland who could do it.' I imagined him shaking his head. 'But I'm not convinced they would do it as well, Alton.' There's no answer to that - I suspect it's an excuse, disguised as a compliment, designed to shut me up!

Alton Douglas

OUTING THE IN-LAWS

That's My Business

I got the feeling, when I met my future in-laws, that I was not exactly their idea of the ideal man. They seem to have set their sights on the world's wealthiest man but one sworn to a vow of chastity.

Her mother does like to give the impression of wealth. She employs two gardeners a week and she's only got a window box.

I wouldn't mind but she's just ordered one of those ride-on mowers.

At one time she was determined to have her own roof garden but the people in the flat above were not too pleased.

Her dad is the meekest of men. Geese queue up to say 'Boo!' to him.

It was rumoured that when she proposed to him he said, 'If you think I should.'

At the ceremony he was the one who wore the veil.

Talk about timid! When it came to the honeymoon he asked if the Best Man could go instead of him.

Anyway, they managed to have several children. She must have bought him a very good instruction manual.

The first time I went to the girl's house her brothers were very protective towards her - it was like a cross between a Court of Inquiry and the Grand Inquisition.

Anyway, we've managed to stay together as a couple and our relationship with the rest of the family continues - through our solicitors.

Alton Douglas

OF THIS AND THAT

(AND ESPECIALLY THAT)

That's My Business

Jo and I went regularly to quite a mixture of jazz concerts. Over the years we saw the World's Greatest Jazz Band, Eddie Condon, Ted Heath, Johnny Dankworth, Jacques Loussier and too many others to list. One of them was Oscar Peterson at Birmingham Town Hall in the 80s, giving a three-hour solo recital. Such astonishing, dexterous and thrilling keyboard runs. I was astonished to learn years later that he suffered from chronic rheumatism in his hands!

-.-.-.-

Someone I knew, who suffered with slight hearing problems, was booked to speak at a dinner. The organiser told him that the Guest of Honour was to be Mary Berry. He thought, 'Great, I love her cookery programmes.' So, the week before, he went out and bought half a dozen of her books, with the intention of getting them signed, to give away as Christmas presents. The evening came, he arrived to be greeted by the organiser who said, 'Come over and meet our Guest of Honour.' He crossed the room to be confronted with a plump, elderly man, wearing a chain of office, who said, 'I'm very pleased to meet thee - I'm Mayor o' Bury.'

-.-.-.-

While I was away on summer season Jo had to employ a builder for a few days. One morning he arrived in a terrible state. He'd been at a family get-together the night before, supped too much and was suffering the consequences. Jo sat him down, commiserated with him and poured as many cups of black coffee into him as his system would take. When I saw her I said, 'You are a kindly, understanding soul - I know what I would have done with him!' She said, 'I couldn't let him do any work. Anyway, I let him go home early.' I tried to be understanding, 'That was probably the best thing.' She shuffled uncomfortably, looked at her feet and mumbled, 'And I paid him for the day.'

Alton Douglas

Computers and modern phones can at times be the most irritating of mankind's inventions.

For example, why do so many companies insist that you prove your identity before they allow you to pay a bill? Why should they care who pays it as long as they receive their money?

Secondly, how farcical is it that you are asked to prove you are not a robot - by a robot!

Then there's the 'Your parcel will arrive between 9am and 12.30pm.' You're frightened to move too far from the door in case you miss them. On a par with, 'The doctor will ring you between 2-6pm.' Can't do any jobs - need my hands free for the phone.

Phew! That's that rant over!

-.-.-.-

It is amazing how the world has changed so much. When I was young nearly all of us had a nickname - 'Fatty', 'Specs', 'Skinnny Lizzie' (one boy, at our school, was known as 'Gernommy' because he did look surprisingly like a gnome. Another lad whose middle name was Ewart was called 'The Wart'.) and you wore them almost as a badge of honour. These day parents seem to be involved in litigation if somebody even looks at their offspring in the wrong way. Opinions will vary as to the merits of all that, I'm sure.

-.-.-.-

I was one of the speakers at a sporting dinner at the now-defunct Grand Hotel in Bristol. It went quite well and shortly afterwards I saw one of the special guests, Ian Botham, advancing towards me with an outstretched hand. I was thrilled, he had always been one of my cricketing heroes and I was convinced that he was about to congratulate me on a wonderful speech and ask me, purely as a favour to him, if I could be the guest at one of his forthcoming dinners and --------- he kept coming, to shake hands with ex-boxer Henry Cooper, standing next to me.

That's My Business

When we first moved into our house we employed a painter and decorator who would whistle endlessly and without any semblance of a tune. I was telling a friend only last week and he said, 'You know that American painting called *Whistler's Mother*? Perhaps he's Whistler's father!'

-.-.-.-

Jo and I had a lengthy friendship with Bill Maynard, with visits to each other's houses, Bill booking me as the cabaret act for a friend's Christmas party, visits to first nights and once a trip to see him recording an episode of his sit-com *Oh No It's Selwyn Froggit* during which he suddenly seemed to completely lose it and let flow a stream of invectives, greatly shocking his 'mums and dads' audience. Afterwards I said to him, 'What on earth was that about?" He shook his head, 'I fluffed a line and knew if I didn't do that they would leave it in.'

ELECTION BLUES

> It isn't difficult to notice,
> No matter where I place my vote is,
> The proof is there I know from checks,
> Where no one else has placed their X.

THOSE IN FAVOUR SAY 'NO'

> Politician's brains are wired
> To redact a subject as required.
> Election over and 'Hey Presto!'
> Redacted this year's manifesto.

Alton Douglas

BRUMMIE BORN

That's My Business

As a Brummie I'm once again proud to list a few of the famous actors who have originated from our city:

Brian Aherne: Born in Kings Norton, not far from our first home, he went on to appear on Broadway and in Hollywood films. In 1939 he was nominated for an Oscar for his role as Emperor Maximillian in *Prince Valiant*.

-.-.-.-

Paul Scofield: The son of a headmaster, he was well established for his Shakespearean acting and went on to play many cinema roles. Three times he declined a knighthood but eventually accepted a CBE.

-.-.-.-

Raymond Huntley: Another son of Kings Norton, he is best remembered as a supercilious bank manager/civil servant-type in dozens and dozens of films.

-.-.-.-

Anna Quayle: She made many TV and stage appearances and was the leading lady in Anthony Newley's West End musical *Stop the World - I Want to Get Off*.

-.-.-.-

Charlie Hall: He became best known as a foil for Laurel and Hardy in almost fifty films. In Erdington there is a pub named after him and his biography *This is More Than I Can Stand* was published in 2012.

Alton Douglas

AGE MATTERS

That's My Business

My memory isn't as good as it used to be, but I can't remember when it was.

I thought I was looking great for my age until a pensioner on the bus offered me her seat.

I've ordered a hearing aid but so far I haven't heard anything.

There's something wrong with our bathroom - all I can see in it is my dad.

I've asked the family not to put so many candles on my birthday cake this year. My eyebrows are almost back.

They say that age is just a matter of years. My years are starting to matter.

I'm told that 'White is the new black' - in my case '9pm is the new midnight.'

I still go for a jog around the park and I'm back twenty minutes later - another ten minutes and my breath gets back.

One of my all-time favourite comics, George Burns, quite naturally had a few things to say about age:

'At my age flowers scare me.'

'He's so old that when he asks for a three-minute egg they ask for the money up front.'

'Nice to be here? At my age it's nice to be anywhere.'

Alton Douglas

A FOOL IN THE FOLS

That's My Business

In 1975 I made a very foolish mistake when I agreed to appear as the Principal Comedian with the Fol-de-Rols at the De La Warr Pavilion in Bexhill for the summer, with Sundays at Bournemouth Pavilion. Hugh Charles, the producer and lyricist for such songs as *There Always Be An England* and *We'll Meet Again*, had seen me in cabaret at The Spinning Wheel in Westerham and decided that I would be ideal. He was wrong! I was a patter comic, not someone who looked visually funny - which is really what the Fols needed. Bob Monkhouse told me that he had exactly the same experience in a season at the Playhouse in Weston-Super-Mare when the second comic, David Jason, was infinitely funnier to watch than he was. Our second comic was Frankie Murray who was far more a Fols comic than me - in the Monk's sketch he used to get howls of laughter. By the end of the run Hugh could barely bring himself to speak to me.

-.-.-.-

I was invited to open a garden fête at the beginning of the season, with Joan Mann, our leading lady. Unfortunately, Joan who lived some distance out decided that she didn't want to come into Bexhill earlier that day and declined. I asked one of the dancers, Jan Revere, to accompany me instead and it went off very well. However, Joan's refusal caused quite a lot of ill feeling in the town.

-.-.-.-

Outside the theatre there was an enormous blow-up photo of me and every time I went past it I used to mentally don a balaclava to disguise myself. It was a mixture of embarrassment about the show but more a feeling that I've never lost that I hated pictures of myself. How I wish I looked that good now!

Alton Douglas

EXCUSE THE EXPRESSION

That's My Business

I can't explain why it is but certain expressions prove to be irritating. I'm sure you could draw up a list at least as long as mine!

'End of.' (Why not just stop speaking? The break says it all.)

'At this moment in time.' (What's wrong with 'now'?)

'I know you won't mind me saying this -' (Brace yourself for a devastating insult.)

In the House of Commons the repeated use of 'Mr Speaker.' (Surely he knows who he is by now?)

'Think outside the box.' (Pardon?)

'To be perfectly honest.' (Here's a lie coming.)

'Let's run this up the flagpole.' (Repeat it enough times and you could end up swinging from it.)

'It is what it is.' (Is it? Well, I never!)

'It's just a joke.' (Usually another insult.)

'C'est la vie.' (But does it have to be?)

'Irregardless.' (Not even a proper word or having the saving grace of being an improper one.)

There again there can be the odd phrase you like to hear:

'Please accept this cheque for putting up with me.'

'I have enjoyed your book.'

Alton Douglas

MORE BY CHANCE

That's My Business

I was offered a wonderful part as a drunken butler in *Bergerac*, to be filmed in Jersey. Unfortunately, that very week was the 40th anniversary of VJ Day and it was imperative that I honour a booking at a Black Country working men's club. They had bought several copies of our book *The Black Country at War* and pasted photos from them all around the concert room. I had also booked two friends, Margaret Lowe to sing wartime songs and comedy magician Denis Beards.

My place in *Bergerac* was taken by John Rutland - the name of the character I played in *Muck and Brass*!

-.-.-.-

My first series as the quizmaster/co-writer of the BBC's *Know Your Place*, went out in 1979. By 1982 we had been on the screens for three series. That same year a BBC radio sit-com, starring Roy Dotrice with exactly the same title, hit the airwaves. (As a matter of interest, I actually came up with the title for our show.)

-.-.-.-

In the early 1980s I wrote to Channel 4 suggesting a programme I called *Trailers*. It was a simple idea - I would be dressed in a 1930s-style suit and introduce film trailers from that decade. The following week it would be me, in a demob suit, with 1940s trailers and so on up to date. I received a very nice reply from the founding chief executive, Jeremy Isaacs (he wasn't the good Knight at that time) telling me that he could see absolutely no potential in it, either in terms of viewers or in pulling in advertising.

A couple or so years later an identical show appeared on Channel 4. Now, I'm not saying that the Commissioning Editor for Fiction had ever heard about my idea but what an amazing coincidence! Your thoughts?

Alton Douglas

BRIGHT SPARKS

That's My Business

I referred to the man who claimed that comics didn't have to be too bright in the chapter *Business as Usual*. In some cases that may have been true but I don't think it applied to many of my fellow laughter makers. I'll give you a just a few examples:

Will Hay: A member of the Royal Astronomical Society, he is credited with discovering the Great White Spot on the planet Saturn.

-.-.-.-

Jimmy Edwards: Educated at Kings College School he became an RAF Flight Lieutenant, winning the Distinguished Flying Cross.

-.-.-.-

Bob Monkhouse: Wrote scripts for Bob Hope, Arthur Askey, Max Miller and Ted Ray and was generally recognised as the sharpest comedic brain of his time.

-.-.-.-

Vivian Stanshall: Was a student at Walthamstow College of Art.

-.-.-.-

Tom O'Connor: Mathematics and music schoolteacher and assistant headmaster.

-.-.-.-

Paul Daniels: Trained as an accountant in local government.

-.-.-.-

Bernie Clifton: Radar mechanic at the Bomber Command School at RAF Lindholme.

-.-.-.-

Peter Kay: Studied Media Performance at Salford University.

Alton Douglas

Harry Hill: Obtained his medical degree and trained as a neurologist.

-.-.-.-

John Culshaw: Studied at Canterbury Christ Church University.

-.-.-.-

Tim Vine: A student at Epsom College and now writes all his own material.

-.-.-.-

John Cleese: Taught Science, English, Geography, History and Latin at St Peter's Preparatory School in Weston-Super-Mare (his old school).

-.-.-.-

Do excuse the self awareness but, although I can't claim any great academic achievements, you are reading my book!

-.-.-.-

Despite my ambitions to be top dog there have been quite a few occasions when I've been more of a straight man than a comic. Reluctant though I may be to show me being bested, it's only fair (I suppose) to give a small selection:

Shortly after I had been ignominiously sacked from the Max Bygraves series, for getting shouts of 'More!', I bumped into Bob Monkhouse in the corridors of ATV. He had a reputation for knowing everything that happened, sometimes before it had. He stopped me. 'I hear you're not working with Max anymore. That'll teach you, when you're doing the warm-ups, to keep your trousers buttoned up!'

That's My Business

I was telling my friend, Keith Ackrill, that due to having a big toe that insists on pointing skywards I was having to replace my trainers every few months. He shrugged. 'When you're exercising in future, you'll just have to wear steel-tipped boots!'

-.-.-.-

I must admit that there have been quite a few times that Jo, forgetting she was supposed to be the straight woman, has topped me. In the belief that I'm known as 'Mr Fair Play', I'll give you one example that I may have mentioned before - but I wish she'd stop making a habit of it. We were driving out of Elstree when, just before we got to the exit, a fox shot under the barrier. I said, 'What the Hell was that?' and Jo, quick as a flash, said, 'I think it was Basil Brush's warm-up comic.'

-.-.-.-

Just occasionally members of your audience can be smart Alecs:

'You're the comic that's just been on - have you kept your day job?'

Alton Douglas

Back again to the world of the Working Men's Clubs and the fondly remembered comments by the Entertainment Secretaries concerning the shows and events:

I apologise to the members for booking the roller-skating act on Saturday. I thought it was a female version of The Bachelors when I saw the name The Spinsters.

I am sad to report that none of the acts turned up for the Grand Talent Competition but we didn't let it spoil the show.

When I booked the comedy act of Dodds and Mills, *A Laugh a Minute,* I imagined they would do longer than that.

A reminder to all members: Dress will be formal for the annual Free and Easy.

Our vocalist for the evening was Maisie Evans. What can I say about her that is not true?

I feel I must mention Rosie and Beryl, our two first-time volunteer raffle ticket sellers, who I hope to see back at the club sometime in the future.

Benny 'The Authentic Black Country Comedian' Gornal was the bluest comic we have ever had. Fortunately, none of us could understand a word he said.

There was a big crowd on Wednesday to see the wrestling. To much applause, after a thirty-minute struggle, the barmaids managed to evict the troublemakers.

It was such a shame that Harry Burton passed away at the beginning of the 'Stodge and Ale' evening. He would have enjoyed the Hotpot.

That's My Business

*If you have enjoyed this book,
why not read 2022's offering,
I Look At It Like This?
Visit Amazon to buy it, along with more copies
of this book.*

Alton Douglas

And there's more...
Try 2023's offering
Funny's The Word

That's My Business

Or maybe 2024's offering
Reading My Thoughts

100% 5* reviews

Another brilliant dip-in/dip-out book from Alton Douglas. Lots of anecdotes from his time in show business, including descriptions (mainly positive but not exclusively so) of many well known people that he came across around the clubs and TV studios. Lots of one-liners and funny rhymes to make the sides ache with laughter. Thoroughly recommended.

Another great read from Alton. Enjoyable, funny and he really knows how to tell a good story. Will make an excellent Christmas gift.

I was laughing out loud on the first page. A very funny book full of anecdotes and jokes. An excellent Christmas present.

In a long and varied career, Alton has appeared in almost every UK theatre of note and worked with just about every star name over the last sixty years! He has a tale to tell about most of them, and nearly all (but not every one!) with fondness and affection.

He has a relaxed and easy to read style and if you enjoy hearing about life in show business (warts and all!) over the last sixty years, Alton's latest book of 'Anecjokes' is one that you will like!

The latest from the Midlands 'man of mirth'. Alton's latest book is a cross between 4 hours with Ken Dodd firing jokes at a rapid pace, plus a vast collection of anecdotes from his many nights travelling the workingmen's club/pub circuit. If you've ever been in the entertainment industry, then this book is a 'must have', definitely worth a read.

www.ingramcontent.com/pod-product-compliance
Lightning Source LLC
Chambersburg PA
CBHW052048070526
44584CB00017B/2100